The Little Way of Living with Less

Also by Laraine Bennett
from Sophia Institute Press:

Know Thyself: The Game of Temperaments

with Art Bennett:
The Temperament God Gave You
The Temperament God Gave Your Spouse

Laraine Bennett

The Little Way of Living with Less

Learning to Let Go with the Little Flower

SOPHIA INSTITUTE PRESS
Manchester, New Hampshire

Sophia Institute Press
Box 5284, Manchester, NH 03108
1-800-888-9344
www.SophiaInstitute.com

Sophia Institute Press is a registered trademark of Sophia Institute.

paperback ISBN 978-1-64413-538-9

ebook ISBN 978-1-64413-539-6

Library of Congress Control Number: 2022940258

Second printing

For my husband, Art,
without whom these adventures
would never have occurred

Contents

Acknowledgments

I am very grateful to Charlie McKinney and Sophia Institute Press for their enthusiasm for this project as well as for our temperament series. I am particularly grateful to my editor at Sophia, Michael Warren Davis, whose insightful comments and recommendations really took this book to the next level. I am also indebted to my family and friends who shared with me their stories about downsizing, detaching, and focusing on what truly matters in this life. I am especially grateful to my daughter Lucy for critiquing a first draft of the book. Finally, this book would not be complete without the wise and practical tips from my friend and NAPO-certified professional organizer Jacquelyn Dupuy, founder and CEO of Interior Freedom, LLC.

Introduction

Come to me, all who labor and are heavy laden, and I will give you rest. Take my yoke upon you, and learn from me; for I am gentle and lowly in heart, and you will find rest for your souls.

—Matthew 11:28-29

Do all in your power to detach your heart from earthly cares, especially from creatures; then be assured Our Lord will do the rest.

—St. Thérèse of Lisieux, *Story of a Soul,* "Counsels and Reminiscences"

Our young, laid-back, carefree Californian family arrived at the Frankfurt airport in Germany with a tower of suitcases, assorted bags, and a three-year-old and a six-month-old in tow. We had sold nearly everything we owned to embark on an adventure in a country that was *in ordnung*: highly organized and rule-driven—the exact opposite of what we'd left. What could possibly go wrong?

We were unprepared for cobblestones and what seemed like constant rain. Our flimsy American stroller and our tennis shoes were the first casualties. Our six-month-old crawling through the *alles-in-ordnung* German train while I (rain-drenched) schlepped diaper bag, purse, and suitcases prompted one passenger to cluck disapprovingly, "You look like refugees from some Third World country."

We discovered that we were fairly stereotypical Americans—big, brash, and noisy. We were regularly chastised for allowing our kids to ride the loud plastic "big wheel" bikes on our street—especially during the mandatory "quiet time" from one to three in the afternoon—and to traipse heedlessly through the bushes that lined our backyard. Germans appreciate the details, the orderliness of life, the peacefulness of a Sunday afternoon stroll, and the many opportunities to create beauty in small spaces. Our landlord painstakingly built a driveway, placing bricks one by one, creating a pattern and planting seeds so grass would mingle in a design of red and green. We Americans would have cemented something in no time!

A bit of lace or a child's handmade mobile is hung in the kitchen window for passersby to enjoy. There is order and care for the small details. I once argued with our landlord, Herr Funk, that I could place our furniture anywhere I wanted in the house. No, he objected, "the bed must go *there*, on that precise wall. Do you see where I put the electrical outlets? And that big wall without windows? That is where you put your *wandschrank*." Never mind that we didn't own a *wandschrank*. Herr Funk's mother promised she would find me the obligatory *wandschrank*. She also chastised me for hanging lace curtains in the kitchen window—curtains that had not been hemmed! (And this fact, she noted, she could see from the street!)

Another time, he reprimanded me for allowing my kids to run through the bushes between our backyard and the neighbor's. "How do you know?" I grumpily demanded, whereupon he took me out back, leaned in between two bushes, and picked up a tiny red berry from the ground. "Do you see this berry? It does not simply *fall* off the bush! It had to have been *knocked* off the bush!"

We barely knew the language, and we were even more bedeviled by customs that were surprising and sometimes even unbelievable to our American sensibilities that demanded freedom and individualism. What a lesson for us who value large spaces, big houses, parking lots, big furniture, big box stores, fast food, wide streets and shopping malls. What's more, as Americans we were accustomed to shopping *whenever we wanted*. In Germany, shops were all closed during the quiet hours in the afternoon and then for the night at 5:00 p.m. sharp.

Hardly anything was open on Sunday, and you could not hang your laundry out to dry on that day. Rent was due on the first of the month (no later), and you must not let your car idle for more than three minutes while letting it warm up in the morning.

> These all died in faith, not having received what was promised, but having seen it and greeted it from afar, and having acknowledged that they were strangers and exiles on the earth. For people who speak thus make it clear that they are seeking a homeland.... But as it is, they desire a better country, that is, a heavenly one. (Heb. 11:13-14, 16)

Living and traveling in Europe challenged our worldview, our assumption of American exceptionalism. By reminding us that we were pilgrims on earth, it also brought us closer to Christ. Our comfortable American lifestyle and our comfortable American assumptions were turned upside down. There was no escaping the fact: we were strangers in a strange land.

As new parishioners at the Catholic community on the military base nearby, we had not attended more than one Mass when the Catholic chaplain challenged us to be not merely Sunday Catholics, pew sitters; "What will you do to help out?" he asked. "How will you tithe of your time?" He urged us to sign up to teach CCD or a Baptism class. He also invited us to walk with him after Mass on a weekly *Volksmarch* — miles and miles of hiking with Germans through alpine forests and country trails, punctuated by a stop for beer and wurst at a little hut in the woods. By accompanying us and challenging us to step out of our comfort zones, he helped us learn what it means to grow in friendship with Jesus Christ.

We struggled with the sense of being strangers — not unwelcome, precisely, but not received with open arms, either. Every day might bring something we'd never quite faced before, so we were always a little on edge and alert. We wanted to make new friends but didn't know quite how. All this brought us out of our comfort zone, away

The Little Way of Living with Less

from the "flesh pots" of California. This discomfort opened up a space where there was a possibility of spiritual awakening, an encounter, a surprise. God is the God of surprises, Pope Francis says. But when you are too comfortable, too content with the status quo, you rarely step out of your cozy cocoon to encounter the surprise.

But this is not just our story. It is not just a story about traveling, downsizing, or simplifying, though we share our experiences with all of this as well. Rather, we hope to share with you some practical and spiritual insights related to detachment, living with less, decluttering, and minimizing. We are not professionals in these areas, by any means. Nonetheless, we can share our own experiences and those of others, including tips from a professional organizer whose practical expertise and wisdom grace these pages.

Most importantly, we are looking to grow in virtue—especially in those virtues associated with St. Thérèse and her "Little Way." This book is guided by the insights and spirituality of St. Thérèse, the Little Flower, who assures us that "happiness has nothing to do with the material things that surround us; it dwells in the very depths of the soul."[1] Thérèse was proclaimed a Doctor of the Church by Pope St. John Paul II. She's a saint for our modern times and a saint whose "Little Way" makes us all feel encouraged to seek holiness, no matter how unworthy we feel. She's a saint whose wisdom and holiness encompass far loftier projects than this humble discussion. Nonetheless, we can't help but feel her profound spiritual insights, her simplicity: trust and humble confidence can help us as we meditate on living in this world,

---

[1] St. Thérèse, *Story of a Soul: The Autobiography of Saint Thérèse of Lisieux*, trans. John Beevers (New York: Doubleday, 1957), 86. Unless otherwise specified, quotations from *Story of a Soul* are taken from the John Beevers translation.

making our homes nurturing and loving oases, yet all the while never taking our eyes off our ultimate goal, our true home: Heaven and union with God.

This book is meant for those who seek the peace and tranquility that comes with letting go of stuff that encumbers us and makes us weary and sad. It is meant for those who are looking to live a simpler life. This book is meant for anyone who hopes to grow in love for God and neighbor by living with a little less. It's for all of us who "dwell in tents" here on earth, while looking forward to that eternal city, "whose builder and maker is God" (Heb. 11:10).

1

Strangers and Sojourners

The Rose of Detachment

These all died in faith, not having received what was promised, but having seen it and greeted it from afar, and having acknowledged that they were strangers and exiles on the earth. For people who speak thus make it clear that they are seeking a homeland.... But as it is, they desire a better country, that is, a heavenly one.

—Hebrews 11:13-14, 16

The world's thy ship and not thy home.

—St. Thérèse of Lisieux, *Story of a Soul*, 50

How do you define or describe home? This is a fundamental question for any human to answer, materially, psychologically, and spiritually. We are embodied souls, incarnational beings capable of transcendence: seeking what is above, nonetheless we dwell here on God's good earth. Our home is both here and not here.

We began our European exodus in a small military hotel at Robinson Barracks in Stuttgart, Germany, where we settled in while searching for a home "on the economy"—that is, in a German town rather than on a military base. This proved to be more difficult than we expected. We spent many weeks living in that hotel while hunting for an available apartment. We finally found a picturesque farmhouse (one that served to make us henceforth forever wary of anything "picturesque") in a tiny village named Ruit.

The name *Ruit* was unpronounceable for our American tongues (hint: it is not "Roo-it"), and we were constantly corrected by locals whenever we spoke the name. We had to write it down on a piece of paper to hand to taxi drivers who could not understand us. Our living space was narrow and tall and (regrettably, as it would turn out) attached to a barn that housed actual farm animals, something we were unaccustomed to, having relocated from Palo Alto and the august environs of the Stanford University campus. In youthful idealism and ignorance, we were charmed by the prospect of living next to a farm. Our children would have their own petting zoo!

The antique farmhouse kitchen was approximately one hundred square feet with only a micro-version of stove, sink, and fridge—and, initially intriguing, a trap door to a root cellar. The root cellar soon loomed in my nightmares as a terrifying spot wherein bodies must be buried. The farmhouse was always freezing, and a space heater offered little warmth. We couldn't get our American-sized box spring up the stairs and into the bedroom, so we made do with a mattress on the floor. Mosquitoes and fleas from the barn animals next door attacked us like the plagues of Egypt, and we began wishing we were back in sunny California. "Did you bring us out of pagan California just to die of flea infestation in the unpronounceable Ruit, Lord?"

Banished from the Garden, we are on a continual journey throughout our lives, searching, longing for love, seeking God. In an "ongoing exodus" we mirror the exodus of the Israelites, leaving behind slavery and sin, becoming part of the family of God, heading toward ultimate union with God: Paradise. As Pope Benedict XVI wrote in his encyclical *Deus Caritas Est*: "Love is . . . a journey, an ongoing *exodus* out of the closed inward-looking self towards its liberation through self-giving, and thus towards authentic self-discovery and indeed the discovery of God" (*Deus Caritas Est*, 6).

Every morning, when Psalm 95 is prayed for the Invitatory in the Liturgy of the Hours, the people of God are reminded of the Israelites who hardened their hearts against God and their experience in the wilderness:

> O that today you would hearken to his voice!
>> Harden not your hearts, as at Meribah,
>> as on the day at Massah in the wilderness,
> when your fathers tested me,

and put me to the proof, though they had seen my work.
For forty years I loathed that generation
  and said, "They are a people who err in heart,
  and they do not regard my ways" (7–10).

I used to sigh, my eyes glazing with overfamiliarity, until one day, I asked, "Why do I have to read *this* psalm every day?" Holy Mother Church in her wisdom must consider that I read this every day because I *need* to. God (through the psalmist) wants to remind us of an important lesson—and not just a history lesson about those stubborn Israelites.

Our hearts, too, easily go astray and become hardened. We grow stubborn, without even being aware of our stubbornness. Our fathers in faith were rescued in the most dramatic way. They witnessed God's awesome power—as He sent plague after plague upon the Egyptians—and then passed through the Red Sea and were led by God Himself through the desert. Yet they wailed against Moses for dragging them out of Egypt, and they longed for the flesh pots in Egypt—even though they were enslaved. They moaned and complained:

> Is it because there are no graves in Egypt that you have taken us away to die in the wilderness? What have you done to us, in bringing us out of Egypt? Is not this what we said to you in Egypt, "Let us alone and let us serve the Egyptians"? For it would have been better for us to serve the Egyptians than to die in the wilderness. (Exod. 14:11–12)

In the desert, they were free and everything they needed to survive was provided miraculously by God—daily bread from Heaven and quail for their evening meal. Nonetheless, they grumbled, "Is the Lord among us or not?" (Exod. 17:7).

The Little Way of Living with Less

The salvation story is retold in each of our own lives. Whether we live our entire life in one small town or travel the world, the drama of letting go of attachments, leaving the slavery of sin and learning to cling to God alone, will be enacted for each one of us.

Regardless of whether one sells all of one's belongings and sets off across the Atlantic to start a new life, one can remain attached to one's own vices, to unhealthy habits, and to sin. We can still be attached to our own will, our viewpoints, and our way of doing things. We may be attached to our need for control, for comfort, for power, or for admiration. At each stop along our personal exodus, we want to put down roots—the way our old dog Ginger plops down her rear end and refuses to budge. Or worse, we send ourselves back to the beginning, like a game of Chutes and Ladders. Fear of the unknown or anxiety creeps in, holding us back from flight, from freedom. We want to return to our happy place, to the comfortable place where we had our flesh pots and as much bread as we wanted. Never mind that we were slaves back then.

Though we really didn't realize what hidden growth God was working in us on our own journey, as strangers and sojourners in Europe we slowly began to detach from possessions, habits, and old ways of thinking. We did not, of course, immediately enter the promised land, nor did we leave behind our albatross of attachments. Like the Israelites, we grumbled a lot. At first, we longed for a country where we spoke the language and understood the customs. We missed fast food, shopping malls, and convenience stores open late. Always slightly off-kilter, we bumbled through Germany, ever so slowly gaining small moments of insight into God's saving power and graciousness in the way He leads us along His path.

Though I started out with an attitude that would make Moses want to hit the rock with a sledgehammer rather than a stick,

God in His endless patience sent moments of grace and insight. Even as we were feeling alone, misunderstood, and homesick in the freezing, flea-infested (albeit picturesque) farmhouse, we were invited to join the local German parents and children to hike in late December through the snowy woods to the top of a mountain. We stopped in a clearing as gentle flakes of snow began to fall, and suddenly, St. Nicholas himself appeared, with bishop's miter and staff in a horse-drawn carriage, to wish the amazed children a Merry Christmas! In a country where there were no Toys-R-Us stores, no Christmas pre-sales or frantic shopping, in the quiet snowbound forest, we experienced a beautiful Christmas tradition that called to mind the true meaning of the season. It illustrates the point that happiness is not found in one's circumstances; it instead comes from within. As St. Thérèse reminds us, "Joy isn't found in the material objects surrounding us but in the inner recess of the soul."[2]

Detachment from earthly things is a particularly difficult spiritual reality to achieve, as spiritual writers have pointed out over the ages. As soon as you find yourself detached from one thing, you realize there is an even deeper reality to be grasped. Detaching is like peeling layers of onions—and then you discover you have to detach from yourself, too.

Perhaps that is why we are reminded daily in the breviary and the Liturgy of the Hours about the journey of the Israelites through the desert. They were shown the promised land early on, yet they were afraid to enter it because the people looked like giants. Because of their lack of trust, the Lord let them wander

---

[2] St. Thérèse, *Story of a Soul: The Autobiography of Saint Thérèse of Lisieux*, trans. John Clarke, OCD (Washington, DC: ICS Publications, 1996), 138.

for forty years in the desert. Though He fed them and gave them everything they needed to survive, they still mistrusted Him and constantly complained. They were stubborn and thick-headed, prone to idol-worship, and were testing Moses' patience at every turn. Though the Lord walked ahead of them, leading the way, they still doubted that He was with them. "Is the Lord among us or not?" they whined (Exod. 17:7). Re-telling and re-reading the stories of the Israelites in the desert, we realize our own need to detach from those things, people, habits, sins, and ways of managing our fear or anxiety—anything that might come between us and the path God is calling us to.

Material possessions are only one example, but they hold more power over us than we may realize. Three of the Gospels record the incident of the rich young man who approached Jesus and asked Him what was necessary for eternal life. Jesus relates the Commandments of God, and the young man says that he has kept all these since his youth: "And Jesus looking upon him loved him, and said to him, 'You lack one thing; go, sell what you have, and give to the poor, and you will have treasure in heaven; and come, follow me.' At that saying his countenance fell, and he went away sorrowful; for he had great possessions" (Mark 10:17-22).

When our hearts are filled with our earthly loves, our creature comforts and our material possessions, we have less room for God. Jesus tells us that to attain eternal life we must love God with our whole hearts, our minds, our souls, and all our strength. That is every part of us, each cell in our body striving to love God! Ultimately, unless we detach ourselves from everything that stands between us and Him, we will never be truly happy.

How can we achieve such detachment? Perhaps the answer comes from St. Thérèse, in her last written words: "Through confidence and love."

Wisdom of St. Thérèse

St. Thérèse is truly a saint for our modern world, one we can relate to and rely on for her spiritual wisdom during these increasingly secular, materialistic times. She was born in 1873 in Alençon, France, where she spent her childhood. The Martin family was comfortably middle-class. Thérèse's father, Louis, was a watchmaker; her mother, Zélie, was a lacemaker. The Martins were devout Catholics who raised their children in the Catholic faith despite the atheistic and Jansenist attacks on the Church during that time. But they were not somber, rigid parents. Their home was happy and open. Louis entertained the girls with songs, poetry, and handmade toys. Zélie dressed her daughters attractively and allowed them to play with other children. The family enjoyed walks to the "Pavilion," a property that Louis Martin had purchased prior to his marriage, Sunday strolls in the countryside, train rides, and visits to the city. Warm, affectionate, sensitive, and intelligent Thérèse wrote, "everything truly smiled upon me on this earth," and "already I was in love with the wide-open spaces. Space and the gigantic fir trees, the branches sweeping to the ground, left in my heart an impression similar to the one I experience still today."[3]

Thérèse was not immune to the allure of the comfortable, beautiful life in the towns or in the grand chateaux, the beautiful gardens and fields, and the pleasures of entertainment. "During this visit to Alençon I made what I can call my first appearance in the world. I was surrounded with gaiety and pleasure and was entertained, pampered, and generally made much of.... I must confess that this life was not without its attractions for me."

---

[3] *Story of a Soul*, trans. Clarke, 48.

Yet Thérèse was wise beyond her years. She understood the ephemeral nature of the pleasures, attractions, and many good and beautiful things of this world. Thérèse knew that the allure of these gifts might distract her from her ultimate goal and hope: to be a saint and to be one with God:

> I like to think of the charming surroundings in which they lived and to wonder where they themselves are now and what use to them are their chateaux and their gardens where I saw them enjoying the good things of life. And I knew that all things are fleeting that we cherish here under the sun.[4]

Thérèse echoed Ecclesiastes when she grasped the fleeting nature of earthly pleasures and goods, even as she acknowledged her fondness for these things. Yet she remained singularly focused on her goal.

What lessons we can learn from this saint and young doctor of the Church! We must never despise the many gifts God gives us, but we should always recognize that they come gratuitously from the generous hand of the Maker. We are blessed by these gifts, and they are ours to use and to care for, but never to idolize. And, most importantly, we must keep our eyes on the prize: Heaven.

Tip — From the Organizer

Having a sense of detachment is so helpful when it comes to creating peaceful spaces. Clutter is just a visual representation of delayed decisions.

—Jacquelyn Dupuy, interior designer and NAPO-certified professional organizer, founder and CEO of Interior Freedom, LLC

[4] *Story of a Soul*, 49–50.

Cultivating the Rose of Detachment

1. In seeking to grow closer to Our Lord, to grow in holiness and virtue, one of the first steps we need to take is to look honestly at our attachments—at those things that take priority in our thoughts, our actions, our desires, and our time. Do we tend to worry or ruminate about money or investments, compare our material acquisitions to those of our friends or neighbors? The *Catechism of the Catholic Church* reminds us that when we are distracted in prayer, these distractions *reveal our heart's attachments* and serve to remind us to turn our hearts once more toward Christ, humbly acknowledging our failure to put Our Lord first.

2. We may not need in a literal sense to sell all that we have (unless we are religious with a vow of poverty), but nonetheless we do need to detach ourselves from our material possessions. Can we, perhaps, take some time to go through our basement or attic where stuff accumulates and see whether we can't make a sizable donation to a crisis pregnancy center or to a local Catholic Charities? We can simultaneously let go of some attachments and help someone else in need.

3. There are many simple opportunities during the day when we can practice detachment on a small scale. For example, when a favorite mug is accidentally broken,

or an expensive wool sweater is shrunk in the wash, or a sentimental memento is lost, we can react with a calm, peaceful acceptance. Perhaps this small loss can serve to bring us closer to Our Lord, when we have accepted it peacefully out of love for Him.

4. We all have certain weaknesses—mine used to be just browsing through Home Goods, invariably finding an amazing deal that I couldn't pass up! Instagram has figured out exactly what will captivate me, and the platform sends targeted ads they know will pique my interest! When these occasions occur, can we make a firm resolution to not fall prey to the consumer mentality and to resist purchasing an object or item of clothing—even when the deal seems irresistible?

2

Maximalist 'Merica

The Rose of Humility

*For the lowliest man may be pardoned in mercy,
but mighty men will be mightily tested.*

—Wisdom 6:6

*It would seem to me that if a little flower could
speak, it would tell simply what God has done
for it without trying to hide its blessings.*

—St. Thérèse of Lisieux, *Story of a Soul*, 15

As Americans (and in my husband's case, as an American from Los Angeles, the epitome of that freeway life), we were accustomed to driving everywhere. But when we moved to Germany, we learned to embrace a different lifestyle. Everything was within walking distance. We needed only one car because most days I walked the kids to kindergarten, to the playground at the edge of the forest, to the *kinder spiel* group, to the bakery and the market, and even to doctor's appointments. Once, I dragged two sick children on a sled through the snow to get to the doctor.

Everything I needed was nearby. Although difficult at first, we found this way of life at once simpler and more peaceful. The German custom of having all shops closed on Sundays encouraged family time spent hiking in the surrounding forest, strolling leisurely through the nearby asparagus fields, or exploring ancient cobblestone villages and castles, often stumbling upon a town festival where we enjoyed their local food and drink specialties.

Our cozy German village was what all traditional neighborhoods in the United States were like until World War II. After the war, city planners and architects in the United States decided that this model was old-fashioned. What we needed (they said) were planned communities segregated by use—homes in one area, shopping in another, schools and churches elsewhere, commercial industry in yet another spot. These sub-sections would be connected by roads, not walking paths. Residential zones are further segregated by areas of low, medium, and high density. Apartments would be separate from townhomes and from single family homes.

A darker influence might be the segregating of neighborhoods by class or race. But if we are to give the early planners the benefit of the doubt, we should acknowledge that everyone wanted to avoid the evils of the Dickensian industrialized city with squalid, cramped, and soot-covered living spaces amid smoke-belching factories and waste-strewn streets.

Today, most families live in the suburbs.[5] The suburbs are considered safe, clean, and a haven for like-minded people: families looking for good schools and safe play areas. Cars, highways, and the post-World War II "baby boom" contributed to suburbanization. The VA and the FHA provided loans so returning soldiers could get mortgages for single-family homes. At the same time, 41,000 miles of interstate highways were being built (often bulldozing once-vibrant neighborhoods and displacing many individuals from their homes) so the main provider for the family was able to commute to his work in the city.[6]

Suburban living usually affords a family enough space so that each child can have his or her own room and perhaps a basement or separate TV room. Suburbs guarantee schools, churches, and shopping within driving distance. Many families—ours included—move

---

[5] Most traditional (two-parent) families. Gowoon Jung and Tse-Chuan Yang, "Household Structure and Suburbia Residence in U.S. Metropolitan Areas: Evidence from the American Housing Survey," *Social Sciences* 5, no. 4 (2016): 74, https://www.ncbi.nlm.nih.gov/pmc/articles/PMC5130094/.

[6] Andres Duany, Elizabeth Plater-Zyberk, and Jeff Speck, *Suburban Nation: The Rise of Sprawl and the Decline of the American Dream* (New York: North Point Press, 2000), 7–8.

out to the suburbs to be able to afford a good-sized house and to be near good schools. The fenced-in backyard provides a safe place for the kids to play. The small towns where everyone walks to school, church, and the corner grocery seem like a dream from the past.

The American Dream of a "mansion in the country," once only the prerogative of the extremely wealthy, was now achievable for everyone. But these mansions are not like the mansions of the past: the stately plantations surrounded by acres of undulating green pastures and horses, maybe a well or a pond, perhaps a few statues, and a grand entrance at least a half mile from any main road. Suburban "McMansions" might take up less than a quarter-acre, situated on a flat, treeless street, separated by only a fence or a few feet of grass, cookie-cutter style. And the "country" is no longer the country, since the farm that once raised cattle was sold to the housing developers.

Although we appreciated and were edified by our four years of expatriate life, we were eager to return to the land of our birth: a friendly, easygoing country where our kids could play in a giant bin of plastic balls while we ate at a fast-food restaurant, where grandmothers cast an indulgent eye on noisy children, where we could buy that big house in the suburbs.

We were leaving behind some hard-won lessons on detachment and small living that we would not revisit for another two decades.

The average home size in 1950 was less than one thousand square feet. Today, the average is more than six thousand square feet. Often to gain the space for a subdivision with large homes, an existing tiny "village" or community was bulldozed or taken over by the developer, who put in new streets and homes. Yet this new "community" bears no relation to the ones they destroyed and replaced. History is forgotten. We discovered this in our brand-new subdivision in a new town whose name was taken from a railroad crossing where the Confederates suffered a defeat during the Civil War. We found the original "town," by now nothing more than an abandoned railroad crossing and a lonely antique store across from a boarded-up, falling-down house.

When we first moved to the new suburban subdivision, we made a sincere effort to get to know our neighbors. On our first Fourth of July, we rented a snow cone maker for the neighborhood kids and invited everyone to bring out their grills to the street and to share sides, potluck-style. Sadly, the event never caught on, and we didn't get to know more than a few neighbors who were friends with our kids. Perhaps this is because there was no true community, no real *there* there. We were just people who happened to live on the same street, a street that was engineered in six months with only a profit motive, as opposed to having been built up organically over the years.

Despite more room for the garden and the swing set, suburban living is not entirely a bed of roses. It is, in fact, a modern social experiment. As one expert noted, there's less a sense of community "than there is in a housing project."

The hurried life, the disappearance of family time, the weakening of generational links, our ignorance of history, our lack of local ties, an exaggerated focus on money, the anonymity of community life, the rise of radical feminism, the decline of civic action, the tyrannical dominance of TV and pop culture over leisure time—all of these problems have been fed, and in some cases instigated, by suburbanization, in ways that few people anticipated a generation ago when mass suburbs were first being created.[7]

---

[7]   Karl Zinsmeister, "A Conservative Case against Suburbia: Are Today's Suburbs Really Family Friendly?" *Cures for Lonely Suburbs and Dying Cities*, November–December 1996, http://syracuse thenandnow.org/NewUrbanism/Conservative_Case_Against_Suburbia.htm.

Why does a subdivision in the suburbs with many large and well-decorated homes and manicured lawns not feel like a real "place"? Why does it not feel like *home*? The British architect Christopher Alexander says it's because "quality in buildings and in towns cannot be made, but only generated, indirectly, by the ordinary actions of the people, just as a flower cannot be made, but only generated from the seed."[8]

The ordinary actions of the people: living near their place of work, going to church, going to school, shopping, eating, playing—all these activities give rise to a little village with a church at its center and gardens and pathways and bakeries and cafes with brightly colored umbrellas, all within walking distance, perhaps surrounded by a forest that softly beckons the townsfolk to enter into its mysterious depths and the children to find an adventure.

The "bigger is better" principle that implicitly colors our decisions and plans is like hidden malware operating in the background, gobbling up usable RAM. And it comes at a price. The price is isolation, unnecessary spending, a poverty of culture, and a huge amount of waste. "Suburbs didn't counter the defects that industrialism had introduced into our communities, they institutionalized them on virgin ground."[9]

Alone in our enormous houses, extended family spread out across the map, our children must be driven everywhere. No longer can you send your child out on his bike to fetch a quart of milk or get himself to baseball practice. What's more, children are isolated unless you make a play date—which, again, assumes Mom can make time to drive him. Worse, our kids never get to experience the

---

8   Christopher Alexander, *The Timeless Way of Building* (New York: Oxford University Press, 1979), 157.

9   Zinsmeister, "A Conservative Case against Suburbia."

freedom and challenges that come from being able to run an errand by themselves, walk to school, have a pickup basketball game, or bike to a toy store. Karl Zinsmeister questions whether suburbs are truly family-friendly in his article "A Conservative Case against Suburbia." He writes, "Children are frozen in a form of infancy, utterly dependent on others, bereft of the ability to introduce variety into their own lives, robbed of the opportunity to make choices and exercise judgment."[10] Teen isolation and boredom—correlated to the growth in suburban sprawl—have been cited as leading to the huge increase in suicide among young people.[11]

Retirement communities allowing only residents fifty-five and older—sometimes pejoratively called "way stations" for assisted living facilities and nursing homes—are a relatively new phenomenon as well. The elderly used to remain in their own neighborhoods. They had the option to walk to stores, church, and restaurants once they could no longer drive. If they could neither drive nor walk, they would be surrounded by family, friends, and members of their church community with whom they have worshiped for decades who would be willing to help. The neighborhood we live in today is a mix of elderly folk, middle-aged retired people, empty-nesters like ourselves, single working people, military personnel, and many young families. The sight and sounds of children's laughter as they run through the neighborhood or ride their bikes is a true joy for us. Is it psychologically or spiritually healthy for people no longer to hear the sound of children playing in their neighborhood and to have as friends only those in their age group? To transplant themselves into a brand-new location where they have to start all over to make new friends and to

---

[10] Zinsmeister, "A Conservative Case against Suburbia."
[11] Zinsmeister, "A Conservative Case against Suburbia."

create a new community where they have no history? Architect Thomas Dougherty and Dr. Randall Smith propose a healthier model to today's popular retirement communities and assisted living facilities, which isolate the elderly: "Today, the elderly leave society when they enter an elderly facility, too often to be forgotten by the community. It is this separation perhaps more than any other single factor that contributes to the suffering of the elderly today."[12] Dougherty and Smith explain, "The concept of 'home,' a place of repose, a place where we as persons *belong* and that reflects who we are as *persons in communion with others,* is one that has been diluted in our current culture."[13]

Technology that enabled us to survive the COVID-19 pandemic with our Zoom calls, virtual learning, and isolation within our homes quickly began to wear thin, and most of us longed for a return to normality. Children were especially impacted by being forced to sit at computers all day with no friends to play or interact with. Community is an essential part of being human. We are not healthy when locked in our homes in front of our screens, even when we have a beautiful, luxurious home to isolate within. Though many sought relief from the anxiety of the global pandemic in even larger homes and with even more accumulation of things, others began to question whether our searching for the perfect home was not, perhaps, misplaced.

We often marvel at the diminutive size of the homes in which our grandparents lived—and in which they raised larger families than ours. We know this, yet we can't close Pandora's Box. An

---

[12] Thomas Dougherty and Dr. Randall Smith, "From Our House to 'Godshuis,'" September 22, 2020, https://www.strongtowns. org/journal/2020/9/22/from-our-house-to-godshuis.

[13] Dougherty and Smith, "From Our House to 'Godshuis.'"

intrepid few buck the system with their tiny homes or ADUs (Accessory Dwelling Units). We read the blogs, marveling at their skill and ingenuity—yet also shuddering to imagine ourselves living in such tiny spaces. We aren't quite ready to sell our homes and all our possessions and take to the road in an RV, squeeze into 250 square feet, or set up a shed in someone's backyard.

Most importantly, as Christians we know that God has made us to know, love, and serve Him in this life and be happy with Him in the next. Our possessions can never bring us true happiness; instead, they often drag us down and prevent us from focusing on what truly matters. When our hearts are encumbered by our many attachments to created things, we have little room to let God in. We are searching for *home*, but we settle for square footage. Our overabundance of stuff is not conducive to peace, tranquility, or raising a Catholic family.

What is the antidote to all this accumulation, stuff, and excess? Perhaps it is to keep our eyes fixed on what is above: our Father in Heaven and the fact that He loves us and has created us for a purpose. That is our ultimate destination.

It is not necessary to leave the suburban sprawl in order to detach, simplify, and create a welcoming home. It is good, however, to reflect on the over-dependence on an abundance of stuff, our American tendency to excess, and our inculturation into a society of far greater wealth than our forefathers and other countries. It is almost in the air we breathe.

Wisdom of St. Thérèse

In 1887, when Thérèse was fourteen, her father took her and her sister Céline on a diocesan pilgrimage to Rome. She had just been told by the bishop that she was too young to enter the Carmelite monastery (the usual age was twenty-one), but that he would check with the superior of Carmel while she was in Rome. He also gave her permission to speak with the Holy Father if she had the opportunity. Though she was very disappointed, she felt at peace because she knew she was seeking God's will. Most of her fellow pilgrims were members of the nobility who assumed her father had designed the trip with the hope that she would change her mind about becoming a nun. Yet Thérèse was not dazzled by these important, worldly people, and understood that "all that glitters is not gold." The pilgrimage showed her "the vanity of everything." "It is in heaven, then, that we shall know our titles of nobility," she wrote about her insights while traveling with the elite.[14]

Before heading to Rome, the group stopped to visit the Holy House of Loreto, which is said to be the home of the Blessed Mother and the scene of the Annunciation. The Holy House was miraculously transported by angels from Nazareth to Italy. Thérèse was not impressed by the huge basilica that was built around the house but rather by the tiny house itself. She said it was like "a casket of white marble around a precious diamond." She continued,

> I am not at all surprised the Blessed Virgin chose this spot to transport her blessed house, for here peace, poverty and joy reign supreme; everything is primitive and simple.... He doesn't want to give us His earthly home, but is content to show it to us so as to make us love poverty and the hidden life. What He does reserve for us is His Palace of glory where we shall see Him no longer hidden under the appearance of a child or a white host, but such as He really is in the brightness of His infinite splendor![15]

[14] *Story of a Soul*, trans. Clarke, 123-124.
[15] *Story of a Soul*, 129, 131.

The Little Way of Living with Less

Living in our contemporary society, we might hesitate to want to incorporate poverty as in Thérèse's description of Loreto. Yet spiritual poverty is a virtue to which we may certainly aspire. Besides, her main point is that we should be longing for Heaven, even as we live here on earth. We should always keep our eyes fixed on Jesus, placing our trust in Him and in God's loving will.

In Bethlehem there is a tiny door approximately four feet high by two feet wide, by which pilgrims enter the Church of the Nativity. You have to bow your head or crouch to enter. It is called the Door of Humility. It reminds us that Jesus—the second Person of the Trinity—entered this world as a tiny babe. And for us to know Christ, to enter into the heart of Christ, we, too, must first become small and dependent. The Little Flower, St. Thérèse, knew this.

With a wisdom far beyond her years, Thérèse understood that even her very desire to become a saint—as great a saint as Teresa of Avila or Joan of Arc—did not come from herself but was a gift from God. Thérèse's desire to grow in holiness, to do great things for God, would be possible only if Jesus Himself took her in His arms and carried her. In her humility, she acknowledges that of her own power, she could not attain Heaven. She could not ascend the ladder of holiness. She was too little, too weak.

To seek the highest realms, to train our eyes to see beyond what is here on earth, we need humility first and foremost. As St. Thérèse explains it, it is accepting ourselves with all of our faults, acknowledging our littleness before God and trusting in His mercy. But this attitude is neither false humility nor is it presumption. It doesn't allow us to give up on our quest for virtue! Rather, it is a very real, very truthful understanding of the reality of God's grace and our cooperation with it. God loves us for who we are—not for our talents or achievements, which are nothing compared to His. St. Thérèse writes, "She knows that nothing in herself was capable of attracting the divine glances, and His mercy alone brought about everything that is good in her."[16]

We cannot climb this mountain on our own, or make ourselves saints, or even begin to love God properly—not without His help. St. Thérèse understood that God's grace was paramount, and so she wanted to be carried to the heights in the arms of Jesus. She wrote about the new invention, the elevator:

> I wanted to find an elevator which would raise me to Jesus, for I am too small to climb the rough stairway of perfection. I searched, then, in the Scriptures for some sign of this elevator, the object of my desires, and I read these words coming from the mouth of Eternal Wisdom: 'Whoever is a LITTLE ONE, let him come to me.' ... The elevator which must raise me to heaven is your arms, O Jesus! We really have to ask for indispensable things, but when we do it with humility, we are not failing in the commandment of Jesus; on the contrary, we are acting like the poor who extend their hand to receive what is necessary.[17]

Remember that humility is a foundational virtue—the word comes from the Latin *humus*, of the earth—and it is the necessary and fertile ground in which all other virtues can grow and flower. Humility is not being a doormat, or putting ourselves down, or being slovenly. It is not thinking less of ourselves, but rather thinking of ourselves *less*. Instead of being filled with ourselves, we are filled with love of God. To that end, we should realize deep within our hearts that everything we possess—our possessions, our talents, our families, our very lives—are dependent on God's graciousness.

---

[16] *Story of a Soul*, 37.
[17] *Story of a Soul*, 109, 209.

The Little Way of Living with Less

So, to seek security in or to take credit for any of these things (whether our image, our abilities, our *selves*) is groundless, and as St. Thérèse said, we must simply hold out our hand and beg for God's grace for everything.

Tip
From the Organizer

The single most important piece of advice I give clients is to pare down their possessions before they begin the process of organizing. Also, that they accept that (as cliché as it sounds) becoming and staying organized is most definitely a journey, not a destination! You have to go into any project knowing that you have to set aside time to keep up the progress.

—Jacquelyn Dupuy

Cultivating the Rose of Humility

1. How can we incorporate into our homes the humility of St. Thérèse—whatever our vocation or state in life—and that sense of simplicity, repose, and communion of persons who *belong*? For example, do we focus a bit too much on making things "perfect" before we invite people over? Can we focus more on creating a place where, as St. Thérèse said, "peace, poverty and joy reign supreme"?

2. In what way does pride prevent us from inviting others in (both literally and figuratively)?

3. Do we strive for great efforts in evangelization or dramatic sacrifices while missing simple opportunities to extend a welcoming hand or generosity to our neighbors?

4. Can we accept ourselves—realistically, not pessimistically—with all our weaknesses and our strengths and cast ourselves more on the mercy of God?

3

Decluttering the Soul

The Rose of Trust

*Truly, I say to you, unless you turn and become like
children, you will never enter the kingdom of heaven.*

—Matthew 18:3

*"And what is this little way you want to teach souls?"
Thérèse answered: "It is the way of spiritual childhood,
the way of trust and absolute surrender."*

—St. Thérèse of Lisieux, *Story of a Soul*, 12

We all have so much stuff. Those of us who live in the First World, especially Americans, need to admit this. A billion-dollar "home organization" industry is built upon this fact. Our housing market is through the roof. Why? Because people want to buy larger homes—and then buy more stuff to fill them with. We suffer from the "disease of more."

Nagisa Tatsumi, whose book *The Art of Discarding* inspired the organizational guru Marie Kondo, reminds us that we used to cherish our few, significant things. We recall our grandmothers polishing silverware or folding a well-worn, handmade blanket. An heirloom serving dish or china set is used only on Thanksgiving and other special occasions. We would use our valued objects as long as possible and care for them, polishing them or folding them away in a cedar chest, or we would repair them. When our valued items can no longer be repaired or have lost all use, we might repurpose them, like taking a piece from the baby blanket and sewing it into a quilt or using the old silver pitcher as a vase.

My mom had a special darning needle, darning thread, and a little plastic foot-shaped sock insert that allowed her to repair holes in socks. When was the last time you repaired a hole in a sock? Why waste time on repairing them when you can get a bagful of brand-new socks at the dollar store? Today, with the advent of mass production, we just buy new things all the time and throw them out when they break or we are tired of them. I remember when the first Target stores opened, filled with cheap, smelly plastic items (much like a Dollar Store) that we assumed were made by political prisoners in some communist country. We tried boycotting until we realized that everywhere everything was "Made in China." And then Target itself got a makeover and began selling more "upscale" items created by designers like Joanna Gaines. These "upscale," designer-inspired goods were also cheap! Even Costco now sells fancy glassware and VitaMix blenders along with giant rolls of toilet paper and five-pound bags of coffee. And of course every strip mall has a Home Goods where we can find Italian crystal or European pottery for Wal-Mart prices. Tatsumi notes that "By the end of the 1980s, the act of purchasing had become an end in itself.... If we carry on like this, we will never be free of the spell that things have over us."[18]

Fr. James Schall expands upon this point when he writes in his jewel of a book, *Far Too Easily Pleased*, "We can see that the purpose of the contemplative life, in one sense, then, is precisely *to keep us from being too easily pleased* with the fascinating world about us."[19]

Why do things have this ability to cast a spell over us? Why are we so easily fascinated by this world? Why do we not recognize that too many things are like too much food—we don't need them, and they can make us sick? Perhaps not a physical illness, but they can weave a web of anxiety and obsession nonetheless, like the power of the ring in Tolkien's *Lord of the Rings* trilogy that leads Gollum to become a shell of himself: a loathsome, slimy, creeping hoarder

---

[18] Nagisa Tatsumi, *The Art of Discarding* (New York: Hachette Books, 2005), 9.

[19] James V. Schall, S.J., *Far Too Easily Pleased: A Theology of Play, Contemplation, and Festivity* (Washington, DC: Catholic Education Press, 2020), 7.

who lives in the dark guarding his "Precious." As St. Paul says, "I do not understand my own actions. For I do not do what I want, but I do the very thing I hate" (Rom. 7:15).

Our obsession with things—an obsession that may be so subtle that we do not see it for the same thing as Gollum's dark obsession—stems from Original Sin.

Fr. Réginald Garrigou-Lagrange says that, in the Garden, Adam and Eve were contemplatives because they were in companionship and conversation with God. They were tenders of the Garden and friends with all the animals. They were in harmony with God, with themselves, with each other, and with all of creation. God walked with them in the Garden "in the cool of the day" (Gen. 3:8).

Their emotions were in harmony with their minds and wills. Eve was never jealous of Adam, nor did Adam look lustfully at Eve. They wouldn't have stuffed themselves with too much food or binge-watched Netflix when they should have been gardening. They wouldn't become hoarders or envy their neighbor's home. Tending the Garden was work, but in a satisfying, fulfilling, and never painful way.

Then the serpent sowed doubt in their minds. Was God truly benevolent? Did He really have in mind what was best for them, like a good father? Is He truly your *friend*? Did He tell you not to eat the fruit of any of the trees? No, it was just that one tree. Would it not be better to have knowledge of good and evil? A shadow fell over the Garden. Eve began to wonder, for the first time ever, whether what they were experiencing in this beautiful garden, what they enjoyed in their original state of perfect harmony, *was enough*.

After the Fall, the original harmony was displaced by a triple disorder that St. John describes as "the lust of the flesh and the lust of the eyes and the pride of life" (1 John 2:16). The first, most serious sin was to refuse to submit to God's dominion: we want to be gods. From that sin, the other harmonies are broken. Our reason is no longer the master of our passions and our bodies. Instead of properly and judiciously using exterior goods, we become their slaves. Christ came to restore the order and create us anew. In a later chapter we will take up the question of spiritual poverty, the evangelical counsel that combats the concupiscence of desire.

Speaking of desire, as I scroll through Instagram, I see beautiful images of chandeliers hanging above tables set with Brussels lace and hand-painted Limoges porcelain; worthy homes set against majestic snow-covered mountains; pantries lined with wallpaper, matching mason jars filled with color-coordinated staples on floating shelves; and immense kitchens with pristine marble counters, drawers instead of passé cupboards, and an AGA cast iron range. Immediately I think less of my own home. I start wishing for something I don't have and start searching West Elm, the Container Store, and Facebook Marketplace. I begin to feel anxious and unhappy, envious of my friends with larger or more beautiful homes. I begin to think uncharitable thoughts. (Is *everyone* selling something on Instagram? Are those home renovation people *neglecting* their own families? Is social media simply about the commodification of ourselves and our kids?) If I am not careful, I will find myself overcome by that "wicked sadness" described by the spiritual writer Reginald Garrigou-Lagrange as stemming from spiritual sloth. And then I will alleviate the sadness by buying more stuff!

"The rich young man went away sad, *because he had many possessions.*"

Instead of seeking the new perfection of home decor, the latest paint color, the perfectly styled kitchen shelves, or the "Instagrammable" life, let's begin now where we are, with what we have. Take a moment to look inward, to search our hearts. What is our heart attached to? The greater the encumbrances, the sadder the life.

It's not about "getting rid of stuff"; it's about making room for what matters.

Nagisa Tatsumi surveyed men and women who all agreed they owned far too many items that they simply did not know what to do with. When asked to decide how best to deal with these items, most chose "discard." Yet they were ambivalent about actually exercising that option, several even negatively associating it with the ancient Japanese custom of abandoning elderly parents in the mountains. Women more often chose "organizing" as a solution, while men chose "getting a bigger house."[20] I know I can relate to wanting to organize first . . . and only with great hesitation: discard.

When our closets, pantries, and linen closets are overflowing, we immediately assume we need special shelving units, a set of matching glass containers, or perhaps some cute woven baskets and bins to corral our stuff. And, under the bed we store the overflow of Christmas wrapping paper, seasonal clothing, linens, and baby items we are saving for friends, siblings, or grandchildren. As a result of all our collective collecting and inability to toss things, the guest room closet is filled with clothes that don't fit and shoes we can't part with. As a last resort (or if we are a man—see above), we decide that our home is too small and we set about looking for a larger one.

In our large suburban home we had a dedicated office that we filled on two sides with a genuine office desk suite: desk, side desk, filing cabinets and drawers, and a large hutch on top with cubbies for every member of the family. I thought this would help us be organized, but I was wrong. Instead, it encouraged us to never throw away any paper at all because we had plenty of space. In our spacious file cabinets, we had all our tax files, our current files, receipts, school

---

[20] Tatsumi, *The Art of Discarding*, 26-28.

papers, wills, my parents' wills, diplomas, medical records, school photos for many years, four children's swimming ribbons and heat sheets from twenty years of swim meets, and much, much more. The cubbies were filled to overflowing with each person's random things they didn't know where to put or simply didn't want to discard immediately: old school photos, holy cards, letters, Christmas cards, keys, ads, catalogs, broken rosaries, newsletters, school papers, seed packets, party favors, gift cards. In true irony, the office began to induce aversive responses. Instead of working in the office, I used my laptop on my kitchen counter. Nobody studied in the office. It became a giant, twelve-foot-by-twelve-foot junk drawer.

Organizing our stuff takes time, money, and space. It postpones the inevitable decluttering that must, one day, occur—possibly by our children, if we procrastinate long enough. Hanging on to things because "it would be a waste" to throw them out is a kind of torture, says Tatsumi.

So, why are we torturing ourselves with abundance? Why do we have a linen closet stuffed with towels, when we actually only need two towels per person—one to use now and the second when the first goes in the wash? Why do we have so many coffee mugs that they fall out when we open the kitchen cabinet door? Why is our garage so jam-packed that we park our cars in the street? Why do we have closets that are the size of a small bedroom?

If we had been from my parents' generation, we might be able to blame the war or the Great Depression. My dad, raised during the Great Depression, never threw anything away: in his toolbox (which I still can't bear to part with!) I found broken screws, ancient keys, and rusted nails. He also saved all of his own father's tax documents from the time he first emigrated to the United States until he stopped working at age one hundred! My mom, by contrast, never stockpiled anything, despite her war-time upbringing, and she lived through the great recession in Germany as well. She managed my dad's "pack rat" tendencies by containing his area of hoarding to the garage.

The moss didn't grow on anything in my mom's house. She was raised during the pre-war economic crisis in Germany and managed to outsmart the Nazis not once, but twice. The first time, she faked appendicitis to avoid being sent to a munitions factory (she actually had what she dubbed her "political appendix" surgically removed), and the second time, she survived an SS interrogation in Vienna, promising to return to Berlin on the next train. Instead, she went to Donau Beach with a girlfriend.

She was frugal, organized, no-nonsense, and efficiency-minded, both by temperament and culture. Books were moved out on a regular monthly rotation to the used bookstore, clothing went to Goodwill, and miscellaneous objects were gifted to family and friends. She was a minimalist at heart. I was fond of the antique Turkish copper pot that my mom kept umbrellas in, and I had secretly hoped to persuade her to give it to me. One day I noticed it wasn't in its usual place, and I asked about it. "Oh, I gave it away to your cousin," she said blithely. That's how I learned to speak up if I wanted to be on the recipient list.

I didn't seem to have the same gift. Clutter spawned clutter babies at my house. I was easy prey to the "home organization" industry and enthusiastically purchased plastic tubs and drawers, multiple laundry baskets of varying shapes and sizes, cubbies, chests of drawers, bins, carts, woven baskets, jars, containers, and storage trunks—to no avail. Our two-car garage was filled with everything but cars, and our basement was the storage unit for all our kids' childhood trophies, mementos, books, and furniture. Selling the childhood home is one way (perhaps a bit too drastic) to deal with this!

When I had to sell my parents' home, I marveled that my mom (who had managed the bills) had only one small mid-century modern teak desk. A single drawer in that desk was dedicated to the current bills. No file cabinets, no overflowing cubbies, no nonsense. My mom was a minimalist before there was such a thing. She understood the fundamental principles of creating an organized and well-functioning home—principles that today's young homemakers are just now rediscovering.

Marie Kondo, via her bestselling book *The Life-Changing Magic of Tidying Up*, became a household name and a television sensation in part because the contemporary world has lost the traditional knowledge of homemaking from older generations, as well as because her method turned popular strategies on their head. She told us that organizational experts were "hoarders" and that we should aim for perfection instead of just taking one room at a time. But her most memorable dictum is that we should cherish every object we own. Our possessions should "spark joy." Let go of everything else and then put things away *where they belong*.

But first, we must begin by discarding. We simply have too much stuff.

Set yourself a time limit or an expiration date. If you haven't used an item in six months or a year, it gets thrown out, recycled, or donated. If you have multiple versions of a useful object, donate the extras. Broken items (even if you are sentimentally attached) are thrown away. If you have items that are sentimental but useless, you can box them up and, if you haven't thought about them in six months or so, donate the box. Though it requires an initial expenditure of time, ultimately living with less is a way to save money, time, and space. It also bestows on our dwelling a sense of order and peace.

Keep only what "sparks joy" or what is necessary and useful, as well as those items that are beautiful and well-made. Go through all your things and eliminate all broken items, duplicates, unnecessary papers (like taxes going more than seven years back), silly sentimental items (tickets to a rock concert or maps from cities you explored during college), journals or diaries you have absolutely no intention of ever reviewing, and clothing you don't fit into or never wear.

Each item you retain must "spark joy" for you in some way. It may be exceptionally beautiful or have significant memories or be essential for daily living. We have in our home many beautiful religious paintings and statues that inspire us to reflect, even if just for a moment, on Jesus or the Blessed Mother or the angels. Similarly, there are items from my deceased parents that remind me of them, in a way that reminds me of the communion of saints and of our hope to be one day reunited with our loved ones in Heaven, at that heavenly wedding feast. And there are the more mundane items that are, nonetheless, essential to your particular home — for example, the French press or the Chemex coffee maker.

Plato can actually explain this joy-sparking phenomenon: he believed that to act well, before you can begin on a goal — for example, decluttering — you need to have an image of the noble or the beautiful. Because we perceive our goal as beautiful, we embark on a virtuous task.

If this is not motivation enough, St. Thérèse provides the motivation to give up our excess stuff: focus on what will bring us true joy, lasting happiness. She asserts, "Only in heaven would I know unclouded joy."[21]

Even more importantly than our homes, our souls, too, can suffer from clutter — the clutter of our sins and attachments. I am reminded of St. Teresa of Avila's description of the soul who lives in the outer court of the interior castle, surrounded by snakes, vipers and wild beasts — incapable of entering within himself.[22]

---

[21] *Story of a Soul*, 31.

[22] Teresa of Avila, *Interior Castle* (New York: Doubleday, 1989), 31.

This poor fellow spends all his time outside of the most important part of himself, that place where God dwells in holy light in the interior of his soul. As we clear out our cupboards and drawers, sweeping away the dust bunnies and scrubbing the countertops, letting go of years of accumulated junk, so, too, we need to clear out of our lives and our souls all that does not lead us to God, so that our hearts will remain centered on God alone.

Clearing out the dusty, dank closet of our soul can be a little terrifying! "There is hardly a man or woman in the world who has not got some corner of self into which he or she fears to venture with a light," writes the spiritual author Frederick William Faber.[23] We will have to admit to failings and acknowledge that part of ourself that we dislike; we may have to take steps to change or else remain uncomfortable with our conscience.

What happens, though, when we do not grapple with it—when we leave the dust and dirt to accumulate? We are likely to become more prideful, vain, slothful, or materialistic and less truthful, as we gradually close our eyes to the truths that God wishes to reveal to us. We need to return again and again to the healing sacrament of Penance, where we humbly admit our faults and sins and commit to amending our lives. Renewed and strengthened by the grace of Christ in our souls, we become "like living stones" letting ourselves "be built into a spiritual house" (1 Pet. 2:5).

Wisdom of St. Thérèse

As a young girl, Thérèse was sensitive, affectionate, emotional, bright, and even headstrong. She loved her home, appreciated

---

[23] Frederick William Faber, *Spiritual Conferences* (Rockford, IL: TAN Books, 1978), 138.

the comforts of the middle-class lifestyle,[24] and loved her walks in nearby fields full of flowers. She enjoyed having beautiful objects, art, and precious things. In fact, her room was rather cluttered!

"I set myself up in Pauline's old painting room and arranged it to suit my taste. It was a real bazaar, an assemblage of pious objects and curiosities, a garden and an aviary."[25] She goes on to detail the many items: a cross, drawings, a portrait of Pauline, a decorated basket with herbs and flowers, schoolbooks, statues, candles, more baskets, boxes, doll furniture, plants, and a bird cage with so many birds it annoyed their visitors.

During her visit to Alençon at age ten, she was "surrounded with gaiety and pleasure and was entertained, pampered and generally made much of."[26] She appreciated the beauty and the comforts of such a life, yet recall that, even as a very young girl, she realized that "only in heaven would I know unclouded joy."

Several times Thérèse notes in her autobiography the contrast between the world that she left behind and her present life tucked away in the humble convent. The intensity of her longing for Heaven, which gave her "perfect happiness" throughout most of her life, never abated. As many saints have experienced, Thérèse also went through a terrible "dark night" of the soul during her final months of life, when the joy of that thought of Heaven was taken away. Nonetheless, she never ceased to love God, clinging to Jesus, praying with great hope throughout the darkness, and behaving in a joyful and loving way with the sisters. "I no longer have any great desires except that of loving to the point of dying of love."[27]

---

[24] Her father was a successful watchmaker, and their home was comfortably middle-class.

[25] *Story of a Soul*, 98.

[26] *Story of a Soul*, 49.

[27] *Story of a Soul*, 198.

The Little Way of Living with Less

In his retreat guided by St. Thérèse, Fr. Jacques Philippe writes that trust or a "humble confidence in God" characterizes the essence of her Little Way.[28]

Shortly before St. Thérèse's death on September 30, 1897, her sister Pauline (Sr. Agnes) wrote: "I asked her in the evening during Matins what she understood by 'remaining little before God.' She answered, 'It is to recognize our nothingness, to expect everything from God, as a little child expects everything from his or her father; it is not getting worried or upset about anything.'"[29]

Tip From the Organizer

It's human nature that we are more likely to keep (or buy) something that we have physically touched. Marketers have capitalized on this fact with samples of products and test drives. When clients are having a hard time letting go of things, I offer to hold up the objects they're trying to make decisions about. Not physically touching each object makes decisions easier. Enlist the aid of a friend or family member in this task!

—Jacquelyn Dupuy

---

28 Jacques Philippe, *The Way of Trust and Love: A Retreat Guided by St. Thérèse of Lisieux* (New York: Scepter Publishers, 2012), 67.
29 Philippe, *The Way of Trust and Love*, 37–38.

Cultivating the Rose of Trust

1. Reflect on the passage from the Gospel where Our Lord tells us not to worry—to be like the "birds of the air" and the "lilies of the field" (Matt. 6:25–34). Do we truly believe what Jesus is saying here? All is in God's loving hands! We do not need to worry or have anxiety about our material well-being!

2. What is our image of God the Father? Is He the loving Father who would never hand His child a stone when he asked for bread (Matt. 7:9)? Or do we need, instead, to worry about finances, stockpile possessions, and suffer anxiety about the future—because we do not sufficiently trust God or because we have a distorted image of God? I am not saying that we cannot have a savings account or plan for the future (we aren't quietists, and we should exercise prudence), but these aspirations should not dominate our worldview, and we should realize that ultimately, we are not in charge.

3. Let's meditate on the idea that trust, or humble confidence in God, can draw down God's graces. This is a truly powerful insight, and we might be tempted to think it is mere hyperbole. Yet if we imagine the opposite—disdain for or disbelief in God's power along with prideful self-reliance—we can understand more readily how the latter attitude would be in some sense

repellant of God's graces. How can we become more trusting in God and less dependent on our own power and capabilities?

4. Can we abandon ourselves to God's loving providence? Or do we want to take control of the situation to ensure that we are well provided for? Abandonment to divine providence requires the humility of acknowledging that we can do nothing good on our own: all is a gift from God.

4

Interior Freedom

The Rose of Receptivity

He brought me forth into a broad place; he delivered me, because he delighted in me.

—2 Samuel 22:20; Psalm 18:19

I am much happier in Carmel, even though I suffer spiritual trials and the ordinary inconveniences of life here, than I ever was outside where I wanted for nothing and enjoyed all the comforts of home.

—St. Thérèse of Lisieux, *Story of a Soul*, 86

When we downsized from 4,000 square feet to 1,500, and then downsized yet again to 1,100 square feet, many friends asked me, "So what size storage unit did you get?" But the point is not to "downsize plus" — that is, have a small apartment plus a storage unit. The point is actually to rid ourselves of our excess.

My husband and I had had a revelation prior to our first downsizing. When we were at home in our McMansion, we spent the majority of our daily life in only three rooms: the kitchen, the living room, and the bedroom. After all the kids had moved out, we were utilizing perhaps 10 percent of the total space in the house. Yet we still needed to repair the giant roof, caulk the leaks, dust the unused rooms, and keep everything clean. Furthermore, Art spent an inordinate amount of time cramped in his tiny Honda, commuting to work. We began to entertain the thought that perhaps it was time to sell the family home.

A realtor friend of mine told me that the idea of "aging in place" (where retirees stay in the family home instead of downsizing) is a bad idea. She said they should sell their family homes and free up the market for a young, growing family who needs a bigger house. This is a radical and unique idea! When we "age in place," we are failing to gracefully step aside for the younger generation. In a more mystical version, laid out in *The Abundance of Less*, a young Japanese potter with very little money describes how he needed to find a new place to live. As he was riding his motorbike through the countryside, he saw a beautiful old mansion. As he approached the house, an extremely old man said, "Ah, you have come. I have been waiting for you." Despite the fact that San Oizumi had just arrived at that spot, purely by accident, the old man mysteriously pronounced: "You have come because you are to live in this house."[30] That was twenty-five years earlier. The potter, whose work is now known around the world, lives in the two-hundred-year-old mansion with his wife and three children.

We enjoyed many good years in our large home out in what used to be the countryside of Virginia as we raised our kids. When one is raising teenage boys, there is nothing better than having a large gathering space where everyone can safely assemble under the semi-watchful eyes of the parents. Many a loud rock band practice was made possible by the existence of the basement and the suburban neighborhood. Nobody complained. In fact, just two houses down the street, we could hear a neighbor practicing on his drum set. Our kids were close to school and friends, and driving everywhere was simply a part of the air we breathed. Most of all, we loved our dining room. Even after the kids had grown and moved into their own homes or apartments, once a week we had big family gatherings in the formal dining room.

Today my husband and I appreciate the fact that we never really lose anything that can't be found within about ten minutes; we love the ease of tidying up and the relief of not having boxes and more dusty boxes of accumulated stuff just lurking in the darkness of the basement! Nonetheless, we also acknowledge that having more guests at one time or hosting large dinner parties is more

---

[30] Andy Couturier, *The Abundance of Less* (Berkeley: North Atlantic Books, 2017), 4.

of a challenge. It was a great pleasure for us to have Sunday dinners with the grandkids or to host Thanksgiving and Christmas gatherings. We are now more limited in our capacity, but we have become (we hope!) more creative!

One of the paradoxes of our faith and of our lives as Christians in the world is that the beautiful, fascinating world that is God's gift to us, a truly awesome universe that causes us to catch our breath and praise the Creator for His extravagant generosity, is not our home. The very world we find so compelling, the only home we know and love, is neither the source of our happiness nor our ultimate destination. Strive as we might to make our external space as expansive as possible, it will have little impact—and possibly even a negative impact—on our sense of interior freedom and peace. The physical space in which we live has little to do with the interior freedom we need in order to love and to find happiness.

Exterior freedom is significant, of course, but one can still be fundamentally free, even though constrained exteriorly. We can be externally constricted, even imprisoned, yet internally free. So many spiritual writers and saints have attested to this. In a very moving recounting of the unjust imprisonment of St. John of the Cross (poignantly written by St. Teresa Benedicta of the Cross, who was herself taken to Auschwitz and gassed along with several hundred fellow Jews), Edith Stein relates how John experienced the "sweetness of the cross."[31] She describes how for nine months St. John was confined to a tiny space, ten feet long and six feet wide, with no window or air vent other than a tiny slit high on one wall. He endured beatings, humiliations, and the deprivation of sacraments with silent, loving patience. Nonetheless, as Edith Stein

---

[31] Edith Stein, *The Science of the Cross*, trans. Josephine Koeppel, O.C.D. (Washington, DC: ICS Publications, 2002), 27.

writes, "The stanzas of the *Dark Night* and *The Spiritual Canticle*, which were composed in prison, give testimony to a rapturous union. Cross and night are the way to heavenly light: that is the joyful message of the cross."[32]

Another profound testimony is the number of years Fr. Walter Ciszek spent while imprisoned in Siberia and later in solitary confinement in Leningrad. From the time he was a young seminarian in his early twenties, he was on fire to serve the Russian people as a missionary. Not two years after he entered Russia, he was arrested as a spy, tortured, and sent to the infamous Lubianka Prison for six years, most of which he spent in solitary confinement. Of his twenty-three years inside the Soviet Union, fifteen of those years were spent in prison. Yet his mission was not, despite appearances, a failure. As he himself came to understand through his painful imprisonment, nothing can destroy our most fundamental freedom: the freedom of our soul.

Inner freedom is not a matter of physical space, but rather it is an interior disposition. This interior freedom depends on the Holy Spirit. "The wind blows where it wills, and you hear the sound of it, but you do not know whence it comes or whither it goes; so it is with every one who is born of the Spirit" (John 3:8).

A friend of mine describes the wild and scary process of discerning whether she and her husband should sell their home of twenty years — the only home their daughter has ever known — and leave their thriving businesses and friends in Virginia to move to a place in the northeast they had fallen in love with. But what about the weather! The ties to Virginia! Their daughter's friends! And, most importantly, the fact that their infant son is buried in Virginia. They felt drawn by the Holy Spirit to make this move,

---

[32] Stein, *The Science of the Cross*, 31.

a feeling that was aided by the fact that Joe had experienced a life-threatening medical situation that made the question of what they wanted for their lives all the more urgent. But one day, while praying in the Adoration Chapel of their parish, Joe heard a voice clearly say, "It's okay to go, Daddy. Mama Mary will take care of me."

As we explore the paradox, it seems that the more we detach from (without despising) creatures, the greater our interior freedom grows. The less noisy we are in our prayer, the less we demand that *our* will be done, the less attached we are to our own goals, desires, and comforts, the more we can hear in our hearts the voice of God, who will give us His very peace. And sometimes, the very simple act of getting rid of accumulated possessions makes us feel more free.

In our case, we had about twenty years of accumulated possessions—including deceased parents' memorabilia and furniture, four grown kids' childhood mementos and furnishings, and our own stash of stuff (including the world's largest junk drawer, remember?), along with all the supersized furnishings it takes to fill a large suburban home. How was I going to let go of all this? It seemed to me that melancholia shrouded our home like a black cloud. How could I think of selling the home our kids had spent so much of their lives in? Trips down memory lane derailed my attempts to separate items we would keep from items that would be donated, sold, or otherwise disposed of. At first, every piece of furniture—the solid wood bunkbeds that were such a huge purchase for us when we were a young family, the first-grade artwork, or the collection of sports trophies the kids had acquired—were occasions to reminisce and to wallow in sentimentality. We couldn't believe our kids didn't want to keep these things! Their value seemed to increase even as I needed it to decrease.

The Little Way of Living with Less

Our two-car garage was stuffed with World War II steamer trunks, paintings, and book collections that belonged to my parents, bikes and skateboards, roller blades and hula hoops, beach toys, boxes of tools, camping equipment, tents, file cabinets, cans of paint, shelving, gardening tools, shovels, seeds, bulbs and fertilizers, tomato cages, cleaning supplies, lawn mowers, wheelbarrows, and toxic pesticides of all kinds. Just looking at the mess exhausted me.

And that was just the garage. I dare not tell you what was down in our basement.

Full disclosure: the plagues were necessary to get us to leave.

The first plague involved rodents. It was a relatively minor plague, through which I learned a few lessons on the hazards of too much stuff. I discovered that a family of mice had been making themselves at home and prospering in our very large kitchen pantry. The Very Large Kitchen Pantry is one of the must-haves, along with a Very Large Kitchen Island, in the Very Large (Preferably Open Concept) Suburban Kitchen. Never mind that our mothers and grandmothers made home-cooked meals from scratch for ten kids relying on only a few small cupboards.

After a short session of hysterical screaming, I began taking everything out of the pantry to clean the shelves thoroughly. I discovered many expired cans and jars of food. I realized that *having a fully stocked pantry*, though comforting, was actually not necessary given that we weren't even making use of the items therein. I took everything out and threw out the expired cans from the time we were preparing for Y2K and donated items we would never eat, like ten cans of chili set aside for the zombie apocalypse. I scrubbed the shelves and then painted them white. With a blank slate, I put back only those items I planned to use in the very near future. Seeing the pantry clean and uncrowded proved refreshing and calming. Plus, any future mouse would not find a hiding place behind overstuffed shelves. I learned that I didn't need to buy twelve cans of anything.

The next four plagues involved water (and other liquids) where it should not be. Both the water heater and the front-loader washing machine dumped their entire water contents into the basement, which then required water remediation from our insurance. God was just warming up with those. We chuckled indulgently about how inordinately pleased we were with our home insurance that paid for repairs, new carpeting, and paint. I believe we might have imprudently high-fived each other about how we got a "free" paint job out of it. A fool and his money are soon parted.

The next plague would test both home insurance and us.

We went downstairs to discover the new carpet was drenched. And it was drenched in … Oh, please God, no!

Our bathtub — and in fact the entire bathroom — was filled with sewage. It had overflowed into the basement. More hysterical screaming before calling the remediation crew. It turns out — news flash! — homeowners are responsible for the sewer line from the house to the street. It had to be replaced entirely at a fabulous expense, not covered by home insurance (because, duh, it's outside and underground!). The entire front lawn was dug ten feet down and four feet wide with heavy machinery, and the basement floor needed to be jack-hammered to expose the sewer line.

Life eventually returned to normal, and we began to think all was well with the world. Then our front lawn began sinking. I thought at first that this was a normal process — the lawn is simply settling, after having had a ten-foot trench dug in it, right? I optimistically purchased a few bags of dirt and added dirt and grass seed. The grass began to grow in, but the lawn continued to sink. Now it was about two feet lower than the rest of the lawn. We doubled down and this time ordered an entire dump truck of dirt from our local nursery and more grass seed. When the lawn continued to sink lower and lower, we began to suspect that we were being visited by the fourth plague: a sink hole. Thankfully, I had purchased "water and sewer line insurance" from our utility company and we were able to have the lawn trench re-installed and examined. It turned out there was a faulty connecting piece: the line needed to go from under the house to the side of the house and then to the street, so it involved some turns and connections. Things began to look up.

Our formerly stunted magnolia tree suddenly began blossoming and growing, seemingly right before our eyes. We marveled, but we should have been suspicious. We got a huge water bill, saying we used the amount needed to fill several swimming pools several times over—in one month. And the water company wanted payment. We told them we had no idea where the water was going! If we weren't using it, why did we have to pay for it? They did not budge. There was no forgiveness for this waste of good county water.

Then our neighbor came running over to inform us that there was a gushing spring that was flooding both our yards. It turned out that in the process of putting in the new sewer line, the workmen had accidentally "nicked" the delicate water line that ran along the same general track. So now we had a new water line installed as well.

Though we had decided in theory that we were going to sell the house, this final plague prompted us to begin taking the necessary steps. Everything was repainted, new carpets were installed, plumbing was inspected, water lines were repaired, and the words "water" and "flood" were banished from our speech. We did not wish to receive any further signs from God. I told Him that I understood quite well and He needn't keep emphasizing His point.

We spent weeks organizing, selling, donating, and making trips to the dump. We learned to let go of books we never re-read but had dragged with us across decades and continents. It was helpful to keep in mind the research study that showed how we over-value our own stuff. Using the "Offer Up" app taught me to look at my supposedly valuable stuff through different eyes. The opportunity to help a struggling young family by taking the offered (lower) price and then throwing in something additional was gratifying.

It isn't the size of the house that changed our attitude, but rather the realization that the stuff we accumulated, the long commute, and the big empty house were unnecessary attachments that had accumulated to the point of becoming road blocks in our own spiritual life. We thought we needed all these things — and letting go opened up the door for more interior freedom.

Wisdom of St. Thérèse

St. Thérèse felt called to be both missionary and martyr. "I should like to wander through the world," she announced, "preaching Your Name and raising Your glorious Cross in pagan lands. But it would not be enough to have only one field of mission work.... I want to be a warrior, a priest, an apostle, a doctor of the Church, a martyr."[33] She wanted to suffer all the martyrdoms of the saints: "My Jesus, fling open that book of life in which are set down the deeds of every saint. I want to perform them all for You!"[34]

Yet Thérèse — who had only five years of formal education, never ventured beyond the tiny convent at Carmel, and lived only until she was twenty-four — became a Doctor of the Church, patroness of missionaries, and a second patroness of France. How is this

[33] *Story of a Soul*, 153.
[34] *Story of a Soul*, 154.

possible? It completely contradicts the "wisdom" of the world, which tells us that we need to be highly educated world travelers in order to be members of the "elite."

Retreat master and spiritual writer Fr. Jacques Philippe describes having the wonderful opportunity to visit the Carmelite convent at Lisieux where Thérèse had lived and had written her autobiography. He was stunned to discover that the space was quite tiny and quite unlike how he had imagined. Fr. Jacques saw "a little provincial Carmelite convent, not outstanding for its architecture, a minuscule garden, a small community" with a hayfield the size of a "pocket handkerchief."[35] Yet, he explains, this was in keeping with the saint's character. "When you read Thérèse's writings," he says, "you never get the impression of a life spent in a restricted world, but just the opposite.... Thérèse lives in very wide horizons."[36]

St. Thérèse understood that her physical confinement to the convent, though it deprived her of some of the worldly pleasures she had enjoyed, allowed her heart to remain free to love God with her entire being: "When I am a prisoner in Carmel and trials come my way and I have only a tiny bit of the starry heavens to contemplate ... I shall easily forget my own little interests, recalling the grandeur and power of God, this God whom I want to love alone."[37]

Fr. Jacques tells us that living in the present moment is absolutely essential to interior freedom. Whenever we are fretting about the past or worrying about the future, fearful of what might

---

[35] Jacques Philippe, *Interior Freedom* (New York: Scepter Publishers, 2007), 18-19.

[36] Philippe, *Interior Freedom*, 19.

[37] *Story of a Soul*, 127.

happen, we are not truly present to the present moment. The present moment is reality—where God is present, where grace is to be had. The future is only imagined reality, the past is gone, and the present moment is the only one we can sanctify. God is the eternal present. If we accept His will in this very moment, we will be at peace. And this will set us free. This is precisely the peace and interior freedom possessed by Thérèse: "In the bottom of my heart I felt a great peace, since I had done everything in my power to answer what God was asking of me."[38]

The Holy Spirit had revealed to the righteous and devout Simeon that he would see the Messiah before he died, so he was constantly on the alert. "And inspired by the Spirit he came into the temple" (Luke 2:27) *at the very moment* Mary and Joseph entered the temple with the baby Jesus. Because Simeon was so attentive to the whispering of the Holy Spirit, he was able to witness this momentous event. He was fully attentive, docile to the guidance of the Holy Spirit and to the present moment.

"Perfection consists in doing his will,"[39] says St. Thérèse—and His will is always available to us in every moment, no matter the state or stage of our life, no matter the state of our health or wealth, no matter the size of our home, the clutter therein, or the messiness. At every moment, God is fully present. Even if we have failed many times to seek and to do His will, we can choose to love God now.

Where we are here and now, the present moment, is precisely where God is. Only the present moment is truly real, and God gives us His grace in the present. When we waste time wishing we were elsewhere, worrying about the future, ruminating over the past,

---

[38] *Story of a Soul*, 136.
[39] *Story of a Soul*, 35.

or fantasizing about living in a different world, we are in danger of letting His grace pass us by. We wind up with only anxiety, envy, resentment, loneliness, sadness, and stress. God's presence in the present moment gives us peace. As St. Thérèse wrote: "I was prepared with great care to receive the visit of the Holy Spirit.... Like the Apostles, I awaited the Holy Spirit's visit with great happiness in my soul.... I did not experience an impetuous wind at the moment of the Holy Spirit's descent but rather this *light breeze* which the prophet Elias heard on Mount Horeb."[40]

Tip From the Organizer

Take a moment to reflect on what you want your space to look like after it's organized. Try to determine whether there's a specific category of items that are prohibiting this more than others: are there too many loose papers or books or shoes and clothes lying around?

—Jacquelyn Dupuy

---

[40] *Story of a Soul*, 89.

Cultivating the Rose of Receptivity

1. What are some ways we can become more attentive to the Holy Spirit, along with our awareness of God's presence in the present moment? Have we set aside a regular time for daily prayer? Do we try to fully participate in the Mass—reigning in those inevitable distractions? Do we try to spend time in Eucharistic Adoration?

2. If we catch ourselves ruminating about the past, worrying about the future, or wishing we were somewhere else, can we remind ourselves that God's will is here, now, in the present moment? Some people find that if they take several slow, deep breaths, they can calm their anxiety and reduce the spinning wheel in their heads, thereby becoming more attuned to and grounded in the present moment.

3. When we meditate on the Passion and Death of Our Lord—the abandonment, cruel torture, and total renunciation of any earthly consolation that He suffered willingly—do we find that we might, perhaps, find a way to cling less to our material things and worldly comforts? Does this not help liberate us from our own attachments and give us a sense of interior freedom?

4. When we let go of possessions (perhaps some of those possessions that are not truly essential for our daily living), do we notice a sense of liberation, of freedom? How does this reinforce the Gospel message?

5

The Only Good Thing

The Rose of Poverty

Blessed are the poor in spirit,
for theirs is the kingdom of heaven.

—Matthew 5:3

And I knew that all is fleeting that we cherish here
under the sun. The only good thing is to love God
with all one's heart and to stay poor in spirit.

—St. Thérèse of Lisieux, *Story of a Soul*, 50

Before the COVID-19 pandemic shutdown of 2020, every First Friday I would help bring the Eucharist to Catholics in the nursing home who were unable to leave their rooms to attend Mass offered by our parish priest. Most of these folks were severely disabled. Some could only communicate their longing for Jesus through their eyes. However, one lovely woman (I'll call her Mary) was mentally alert and engaging, though unable to leave her bed. She told me with a big smile about the time she gave everything away.

Mary had been given a terminal diagnosis and put on hospice. She was given one month to live. Her sons, who lived far away, flew in. Together they went through all her possessions, reminiscing over old times, laughing, crying, and giving everything away with great intentionality and love. "This particular vase goes to my cousin in California, and this artwork goes to my friend in Tennessee." After everything—including her home—was sold or given away, the doctors called to tell her they had been mistaken. The shadow has retreated. She would, like Hezekiah, live.

Now she is all alone, without her home or possessions, dependent upon the good will of those who care for her. She has nothing but a few articles of clothing and a photo album. Yet she told me with wonder and joy, "It was the best time of my life. We were so happy and I was going to meet Jesus." Shouldn't we all live like this? Letting our possessions, our habits, and our attachments slip easily through our fingers, relying solely on God's grace?

Even if we don't actually give away everything, we can cultivate an attitude of being poor in spirit. But what does it mean to be poor in spirit? I read somewhere that poverty of spirit is the entrance into the heart of Christ. Mary in the nursing home expressed her joy and anticipation for meeting Jesus. St. Thérèse's little way of trust and love—always focused on Christ, always counting on Jesus Himself to carry her—is the same poverty of spirit that opens the Kingdom of Heaven.

The Kingdom of Heaven is at odds with the kingdom of this world. We cannot serve two masters. We must maintain our focus on our ultimate goal: Heaven. The spirituality that we learn from St. Thérèse is to be simultaneously aware of our *smallness* and yet *confident*, trusting in God to bring us to His heavenly home and to grant us the grace necessary to do His will.

Thérèse wanted to be a saint—in fact, a great saint!—as well as a martyr, a priest, and a missionary. ("I choose *all*," she said.) Yet, this desire was neither a childish fantasy nor self-motivated pride. This desire sprang from a heart overflowing with love for Jesus. In fact, in complete humility she acknowledged that her desire to become a saint could only have come from God Himself, for she herself was so little. Thérèse knew she could place her confidence in God to achieve this:

> Then I received a grace which I have always looked upon as one of the greatest in my life.... I considered that I was born for glory and when I searched out the means of attaining it, God inspired in me the sentiments I have just described. He made me understand my own glory ... would consist in becoming a great *saint!* This desire could

certainly appear daring if one were to consider how weak and imperfect I was, and how, after seven years in the religious life, I still am weak and imperfect. I always feel, however, the same bold confidence of becoming a great saint because I don't count on my merits since I have *none*, but I trust in Him who is Virtue and Holiness. God alone, content with my weak efforts, will raise me to Himself and make a *saint*.[41]

How do we who live in the world acquire poverty of spirit? We may not be called to live as St. Thérèse in a cloister or to become martyrs or to have otherwise extraordinary lives, yet we too are called to holiness—whatever our vocation is, whether the priesthood or religious life, or to marriage and family. In the end each one of us is called to the vocation of love.

Several years ago, we visited Nazareth while on pilgrimage to the Holy Land. Our bus pulled up a long hill to a dingy, gray city filled with nondescript houses and narrow streets. We saw the Church of the Annunciation and a cave where the Angel Gabriel appeared to Mary. We also got a glimpse of an excavation site that may be the very home of the Holy Family. It was a stark contrast to the beautiful, lush vineyards and verdant hills of Ein Karem, where Mary's cousin Elizabeth lived. St. Nathaniel's question, "Can anything good come out of Nazareth?" seems as true today as it was at the time of Christ. I confess to being taken aback by the cave-like dwellings in which Jesus, Mary, and Joseph must have lived. My pious imaginings of Mary dressed in flowing blue gowns while placing flowers on a beautiful hand-carved table made by Joseph and Jesus were at odds with the fact that Joseph was likely

---

[41] *Story of a Soul*, 81–82.

a *tekton*, or artisan, who worked with stone and whose woodworking may have been for agricultural purposes—a yoke for animals,[42] for example, or beams for a roof. They lived in tight quarters in a cave-like home with extended family—in a poor, backwater town. It helped me understand, too, why the neighbors said incredulously, "Is not this Jesus, the son of Joseph?" (John 6:42).

What do we learn from the fact that Jesus was raised in a poor, backwater town, possibly in a cave-like dwelling, and that He went on to say, "Foxes have holes, and birds of the air have nests; but the Son of man has nowhere to lay his head" (Matt. 8:20)? And we are supposed to imitate Christ, to follow in His footsteps! St. Thérèse wrote to her sister Céline about this passage as she reflected on the calling of Zacchaeus: "This is where we must descend in order that we may serve as an abode for Jesus. To be so poor that we do not have a place to rest our head."[43]

Does this mean we cannot have a home? Or create a lovely home? What does being *poor in spirit* mean for us?

Spiritual writer Fr. Donald Haggerty says that there is no natural disposition for poverty of spirit.[44] It cannot be acquired in a few short lessons because, as Fr. Haggerty explains, "Only providentially, often by events that unmask a deeper loneliness in a soul, can impoverishment ever be welcomed and even become attractive." It is a rich source of meditation—whether on the poverty of Nazareth, the fact that the second Person of the Blessed Trinity has no place to lay His head, or the hiddenness of God's glory while

---

[42] Justin Martyr says Jesus was a maker of yokes, which would have required a highly skilled artisan. Interestingly, the Greek word *tekton* means "maker," which also suggests the Creator.

[43] St. Thérèse, Letter to Céline, *Magnificat*, vol. 23, no. 9, 248.

[44] Donald Haggerty, *Contemplative Provocations* (San Francisco: Ignatius Press, 2013), 116.

He walked this earth and even until the Second Coming. There is one way, however, that we can be assured to learn to value poverty of spirit: by reflecting on our death.

The COVID pandemic has accentuated the fact that as a society we are terrified of death. Our entire world has been willing to turn itself upside-down with social distancing, masks, and stay-at-home mandates to avoid the virus. Of course, at first we really didn't know how deadly it would be. Yet even now that we have vaccines and know that few children are adversely affected, large swaths of the population are still afraid to re-enter the world. Several people told me that, even though they were unlikely to actually *die* from COVID, they did not even want to risk being sick at all! One of my neighbors didn't leave her condo for an entire year—not even to take her beloved walks in the fresh air. Instead, she purchased a Peloton so she would never have to leave her home. I note with incredulity that Martha Stewart at age eighty is doing photo shoots (looking like she is about fifty), creating new businesses, laughing with Snoop Dog, and driving her snowplow. But all this youthful enterprise cannot prevent the inevitable, even for Martha. It is as though our society hopes for "eternal life"—but here on earth, extending the average lifespan to hundreds of years!

We were recently giving a talk at a local parish for their marriage ministry. It was during COVID, so the talk took place outside and the seating was spaced out. We ran into old friends, a husband-and-wife team of medical doctors. The husband told me that an elderly woman in her eighties told him after Mass, "I'm so scared that I'm going to die of COVID."

Mr. Doctor replied, "Why are you scared? You just received Jesus!"

"Aren't *you* afraid to die?" the elderly woman asked incredulously.

The Little Way of Living with Less

Mrs. Doctor interjected, "Not at all! This place is nice, but it's not anything compared to eternal life." Now, these two doctors have the proper supernatural spirit, something to which I can only aspire.

In ages past, there was not such fear, perhaps because the older generations actually lived with the dying. Today we tuck our elderly away in a closet, as Pope Francis once put it. Otherwise, they send themselves off to a retirement community, away from their families.

St. Columban reminds us to "love the things above, to desire the things above, to relish the things above and to seek our home there, for the fatherland is where our Father is.... Unless we are filled with the urgent longing of heavenly desires, we shall necessarily be ensnared in earthly ones."[45]

Paradoxically, awareness of death can revitalize our lives. If you were given a terminal diagnosis and were going to die in six months, you would spend those six months very intentionally, in the most meaningful way possible—like Mary from the nursing home. You may try to live the rest of your life as intensely as possible.

When our daughter and son-in-law were expecting their first child, they resisted the urge to immediately buy a home (despite peers and friends doing so) and stayed in their five-hundred-square-foot apartment. They explained:

> Nick and I came across a blog about a couple doing a "spending freeze" for three months, in which they did zero non-essential spending. We weren't in any particular financial difficulty at the time, but it seemed like a worthwhile challenge, so we decided to try it out. We combed through our credit card statements and canceled all subscriptions,

---

[45] *Magnificat* 22, no. 8 (New York: Magnificat, 2021), 273.

focused on eating frugally and not buying anything that wasn't absolutely necessary. We were shocked both by how much more money we accumulated in those three months, and yet we were no less happy or satisfied with our lives. It was an eye-opening experience that led us to rethinking spending money on a larger apartment. We decided to re-sign our lease on our five-hundred-square-foot apartment because we loved the area, it was walkable and bikeable, and we felt at home.

Through their experimental "spending freeze" they discovered they didn't need as much space as they thought they did. This is a practical, twenty-first-century implementation of "poverty of spirit."

We don't have to give everything away or dramatically downsize in order to live poor in spirit. In fact, we can do all that and still *not* be poor in spirit, for if we do not have purity of intention, all is to no avail. Nonetheless, according to the *Catechism*, we have an *obligation* to live the evangelical counsel of poverty. One practical way to live this can be found in the wisdom of the desert fathers, those men and women of the third century AD who became the first hermits, ascetics, and spiritual directors by leaving the world to live in the desert. Perhaps surprisingly (or not), their instructions are immensely applicable to today's culture! Thomas Merton spoke of an abbot who "frequently admonished his disciple, saying: 'Never acquire for yourself anything that you might hesitate to give to your brother if he asked you for it.' "[46] We can certainly practice this whenever we find ourselves drawn to purchase a new household item, pair of shoes, or adorable knickknack.

---

[46] Thomas Merton, *The Wisdom of the Desert: Sayings from the Desert Fathers of the Fourth Century* (Trappist, KY: Abbey of Gesthemani, 1960), 60.

The Little Way of Living with Less

Wisdom of St. Thérèse

"No, there is no joy comparable to that which the truly poor in spirit experience."[47]

Thérèse was acutely aware of the transient nature of material things and of the impermanence of this present life. Even at a very young age she understood that even those who believe themselves to be good Christians can be overly entranced by the world. Consider this passage from *Story of a Soul*, part of which we read in an earlier chapter:

> I think it is a great grace that we left Alençon, as our friends there were too worldly and too clever at mixing the pleasures of the world with the service of God. They scarcely gave a thought to death, and yet death has called many of the people I knew and they were young and rich and happy. I like to think of the charming surroundings in which they lived and to wonder where they themselves are now and of what use to them are their chateaux and their gardens where I saw them enjoying the good things of life.[48]

Can we be similarly focused and strive to attain poverty of spirit? Or are we satisfied with "mixing the pleasures of the world with the service of God"? Just as Thérèse learned to give up her self-centered and sensitive ways in order to become mature enough to enter

---

[47] *Story of a Soul*, 209. She goes on to explain *spiritual charity*, where in a situation in which someone asks to "borrow" some time from Thérèse, she does not say "here, you may have it as a gift." Rather, she agrees to "lending" her time—even knowing the other sister will never be able to return the favor—because that is the harder thing to do for Thérèse; namely, allowing the other sister to not feel indebted. In this instance, she takes poverty of spirit to an even greater depth of delicate charity.

[48] *Story of a Soul*, 49.

Carmel, we too can learn to detach from our material possessions and our worldly obsessions. Thérèse gives us the clue when she reminds us of the inevitability of our death—death spares no one.

When she was a young novice, St. Thérèse gained a profound spiritual insight from an ordinary experience. She discovered that one of the other sisters had mistakenly taken her lamp. She was not able to ask for it because it was during the time of Great Silence. She was forced to spend an hour in pitch darkness. Yet Thérèse gleans spiritual lessons from this ordinary, frustrating experience. "Instead of feeling annoyed at being thus deprived of it, I was really happy, feeling that Poverty consists in being deprived not only of agreeable things but of indispensable things too. And so in this *exterior darkness*, I was interiorly illumined!"[49]

Thérèse's attention to the very small details gives rise to her profound insight that being poor in spirit also includes the voluntary (and joyful) renunciation of even those things we deem absolutely essential! This prompts us to consider that we, too, might look for simple ways to give a little more of ourselves, even to the point where it hurts, like the Widow in Mark 12:41–45. Perhaps donate more money than we had set aside to give to the Church or to the poor—even knowing that our money may not always be spent exactly as we would like. Or perhaps when someone asks us to have coffee and it really cuts into our busy schedule, we make the sacrifice to spend that time. And sometimes just a simple smile and nod of encouragement is just what a grouchy, annoying co-worker needs!

On another occasion, Thérèse felt inspired to help a grumpy, elderly, hard-to-please nun. Thérèse offered to leave her evening prayers to bring the elderly nun to the refectory. She could do nothing right for the old woman: she complained that Thérèse

---

[49] *Story of a Soul*, 154.

was moving either too quickly or too slowly, the old nun would fear she was falling, and she thought the young novice was far too young to care for her. Yet always Thérèse would offer her sweetest smile—and eventually won over the elderly nun.

> One winter evening I was as usual doing the humble task I have just described. It was cold and dark. Suddenly I heard away in the distance the music of a small orchestra and I pictured to myself a richly furnished and decorated drawing room, glowing with light and containing fashionably dressed young women exchanging worldly compliments. Then I looked at the poor invalid I was guiding along. Instead of music, I heard her pitiful complaints; instead of elegant decoration, I saw the bare bricks of our cloister in a faint glimmer of light…. Our Lord poured on it that light of truth which so outshines the false glitter of earthly pleasures that I would not have given up the ten minutes it took for me to perform my act of charity in exchange for a thousand years of such worldly parties.[50]

St. Thérèse saw in a moment the stark contrast between the fashionable, worldly life of pleasure and the bare bricks of her cloister with the plaintive cries of the invalid. She understood that the former was a perishable, "false glitter," while her own life was spent in search of that true happiness, true peace, and everlasting joy that would be found in Heaven. And the Kingdom of Heaven begins, like the tiniest mustard seed or the hidden leaven, unseen within our hearts.

One of the ways we can retain our focus on what truly matters and ignore the "false glitter" is to remind ourselves that we are

[50] *Story of a Soul*, 140–141.

destined for eternal bliss together with the Holy Trinity in Heaven. As Thérèse wrote,

> Ah! what peace floods the soul when someone rises above natural feelings. No there is no joy comparable to that which the truly poor in spirit experience. If such a one asks for something with detachment, and if this thing is not only refused but one tries to take away what one already has, the poor in spirit follow Jesus' counsel: "If anyone take away your coat, let go your cloak also.[51]

Tip From the Organizer

Someone, at some point, will have to deal with your stuff—whether it's you or those tasked with clearing out your space after you've passed on.

—Jacquelyn Dupuy

---

[51] *Story of a Soul*, 209.

Cultivating the Rose of Poverty

1. The *Catechism of the Catholic Church* adjures us that "The precept of detachment from riches is *obligatory* for entrance into the kingdom of heaven."[52] This should cause us to pause and reflect on the abundance we in this First World country enjoy. Can we be more generous in our monetary giving to our parish, to our local food pantry or homeless shelter, or to those struggling with poverty, famine, and strife overseas? Can we emulate the widow who gave out of her own necessity rather than abundance?

2. What might we do daily to practice "practical austerity"? Are we careful with our household items, or do we tell ourselves that we can always buy a replacement? Do we hold on to clothing or kitchenware that we never use, "just in case"? Perhaps we can eliminate those extras and donate them to someone in need? Can we tidy up one room—or even a corner of a room—each day?

3. Do we avoid unnecessary expenditures? Can we implement a "spending freeze"? Do we resist the temptation to create "false needs"? Do we try to avoid indulging our imaginations or daydreaming about luxuries or

---

[52] *Catechism of the Catholic Church, 2nd edition* (Washington, DC: United States Catholic Conference, 1994, 1997), 2544.

other material possessions we wish we had? Do we try to avoid the temptation to scroll through social media and fall prey to ads or to envy of others' lifestyle or status?

4. Have we reflected on what really matters—in light of our inevitable death? How much time do we spend thinking about material needs as opposed to the more important spiritual needs of our souls? Do we spend time contemplating the four last things: death, judgment, Heaven, and Hell?

6

A Place That's Alive

The Rose of Charity

"Teacher, which is the great commandment in the law?"
And he said to him, "You shall love the Lord your God
with all your heart, and with all your soul, and with all
your mind. This is the great and first commandment."

—Matthew 22:36–38

You know, God, that I have never wanted anything but to love
You alone. I long for no other glory.... Love attracts love and
mine soars up to You, eager to fill the abyss of Your love, but it
is not even a drop of dew lost in the ocean. To love You as You
love me, I must borrow Your love—only then can I have peace.

—St. Thérèse of Lisieux, *Story of a Soul*, 147

Tiny-home-living, minimalism, organizing, and decluttering are hot topics today. But what is the purpose? It is often not clear what ideals are motivating the trends. Is it minimalism for minimalism's sake? It is organizing to be trendy? Does our pantry really need matching mason jars with cute labels in order to function efficiently? And what about the all-white kitchen with open shelving or the "capsule wardrobe," or even the non-conformist "living off the grid" in a tiny home or an RV? Is this motivated by noble ideals or is it just for "show"?

Without the motivation of truly *inspiring* goals—to strengthen the bonds of love, to serve others better, to follow Christ more perfectly, to love God with our whole mind, heart, soul and strength—it is likely that we will soon find ourselves frustrated with any decluttering, organizing, or minimizing project. Simply tidying or organizing or minimizing without the motivation of a truly meaningful ideal will likely fall short of the abundant life we are called to as Catholic Christians. Increasing our Instagram followers, impressing our friends, being "successful," or having a "perfect" home are insufficient goals. In fact, I would argue that, whether minimalist or maximalist, big or tiny home, abundance or more or less, our true motivation can be tainted. The goal is not to be a "minimalist." In the end, it really is not about our possessions at all. It's not about getting them, and it's not about renouncing them. This too can be "false glitter," to borrow St. Thérèse's words. The more difficult thing to do is to renounce our own will and to follow Christ. As Pope St. Gregory said, "Renouncing what we *have* is not so much; renouncing what we *are* amounts to a great deal." It is about Jesus Christ and our love for Him. In the end, our goal is the perfection of love—for God, for our neighbor.

We were blessed with many years of raising our kids in a big suburban house—albeit driving everywhere, every day. We didn't really question our lifestyle, since everyone else we knew were in the same boat: days spent almost entirely in the car, driving from school to school to school and sports practice to sports practice to sports practice all over northern Virginia. Once I was complaining to a spiritual director about how much I was driving every day, and he blurted out, "That's crazy!" (In an ironic twist, I had driven an hour through traffic in between sports practices to get this advice.) We all had acclimated to a life spent driving everywhere. We believe it was worth it, especially for the small Catholic high school that our kids were able to attend and our beautiful parish church for which we were honored to be founding members. Eventually, though, it was time to move. Selling my parents' beautiful home and dividing up all their possessions into categories of keep, donate, sell, or trash left a wound in my heart. I didn't want to leave four thousand square feet of decades (and now, generations!) of clothing, furnishings, and memorabilia for my children to deal with. More importantly, we wanted to focus more on the health and well-being of my husband (too much time spent driving in traffic around Washington, DC!), having time with our adult children and grandchildren (rather than dealing with never-ending house repairs), and—one of our major goals—to live within walking distance of a Catholic church.

We decided to move to a historic little neighborhood near our workplaces, a very dense (but not congested) area with no single-family homes, built just as World War II was breaking out. At the time, President Roosevelt had just begun building the Pentagon, the largest defense office in the country, and needed housing for the many civilian and military personnel who had come to the Washington, DC, area to work in defense jobs. Construction on Fairlington began in 1942.

The meticulous architect, Kenneth Franzheim, committed to building solid, attractive, and enduring structures, using only the best materials, despite potential wartime shortages. He decided on combining the architectural style of the colonial period with the newest style: "two- or three-decker garden apartments in a countrified setting."[53] It became known as Colonial Revival. One of the contractors, John Kelly (father of actress Grace Kelly) noted that he used ten million bricks for the project. Eventually, the military-style housing was converted to condominiums and townhomes available for anyone to purchase. It has become a haven for young families just starting out, with its proximity to shopping, work, church, schools, family-friendly parks, and walking paths. It's a bit like a blast from the past when we see kids riding their bikes to the nearby elementary school or playing hide-and-seek in the common grounds.

The recently deceased architect Christopher Alexander, who developed the concept of pattern language, wrote about the "quality of life": "And we must seek it, for our own sakes in our surroundings, simply in order that we can ourselves become alive."[54] Does it seem cliché—or even wrong—to talk about "quality of life?" This phrase is often invoked to cover abuses against the dignity of human persons; "quality of life" arguments are often used to justify cutting short a human life. Nonetheless, there is a kernel

---

[53] Catherine D. Fellows, *Fairlington at 50: May 1943–May 1993*, 11.

[54] Alexander, *The Timeless Way of Building*, 54.

of truth here. When quality of life is put to the service of higher ideals—serving God and neighbor, strengthening our relationships, love—it can be truly rewarding.

Imagine this scene: we are sitting under red umbrellas at an outdoor pizza restaurant, twinkling café lights overhead, sipping beer with the associate pastor, having walked over after Mass. As we are chatting, a man with a marine-style hair cut (high and tight) and civvies hails our priest friend, who beckons him to join us. It turns out he is a military chaplain and lives in our neighborhood.

"Do you have a Subaru with "Catholic Charities," "26.2," and "Zombie Apocalypse" car magnets on your car?" the chaplain asks me.

"Why, yes," I reply, surprised that someone would have noticed these details.

"I walk past your car every day on the way to the bus stop."

It turns out he is our back door neighbor! Since then, we've gotten together several times for dinner, and, in one of my fondest memories, he invited us to join him as he celebrated Mass in his home before he shipped out for his latest deployment.

We often reflect on the fact that our quaint historic neighborhood with its narrow and winding tree-lined streets, undulating sidewalks, hidden pathways, and red bricks (not brick facades) could not be constructed today. It would not be cost-effective to waste valuable land on useless green space, narrow hilly streets, hidden steps, and an abundance of trees. Why waste time constructing homes around all the trees and the hills when the land could be more quickly bulldozed flat? Solid brick homes with slate roofs are surely not cost-effective today. A brick-lined water drain-off canal could be created more efficiently, if less aesthetically. Yet, perhaps then the neighborhood would not be "alive."

"We become alive to the extent the buildings and towns we live in are alive," writes Christopher Alexander. Even living things can be "lifeless" in a certain sense. A neighborhood, a building, and even sometimes a home can be lifeless, soul-less. In addition to (or because of) having the mysterious "quality without a name," our present neighborhood is humane, real, and built around the lives of the people who live here. We live in the midst of more people: people we go to church with and who are our neighbors. Houses are close together (there are no single-family homes), facilitating neighborly contact. We see and chat with many more neighbors than we did in the suburban subdivision, where we almost felt walled-up in our fortress mansions. We can walk to church and the neighborhood bar, sometimes directly from one to the other. It is energizing.

And don't we want our living spaces to be alive and real? In our American rush to be more efficient, get more square footage, and build bigger and better homes, we might have lost a sense of proportion, the actual use we make of our space, and the true purpose of our home.

Sarah Susanka, architect and author of the *Not So Big* series and often credited with founding the tiny house movement, emphasizes the quality of space over quantity. She reminds us that homes are meant to nurture, not to impress. Susanka quotes a couple who, after attending one of her lectures, commented that they just built an enormous home that they hate: "All we've got is square footage with no soul."[55] Size can actually be detrimental to that sense of aliveness in a home. This quality needs to reflect *who* lives in the home and be perfectly aligned. As Christopher Alexander said, part of being alive and eternal is freedom: freedom from inner contradictions, such as the odd notion that a home is decorated or purchased with the purpose of impressing the neighbors. A home is meant for

---

[55] Sarah Susanka, *The Not So Big House* (Newtown, CT: Taunton Press, 2001), 8.

nurturing the humans within, for caring for their bodies and souls, for serving one another and strengthening the bonds of love, and ultimately for bringing each one to eternal happiness in Heaven.

Our daughter and son-in-law felt that walkability was a critical factor in deciding where their family should live. When they lived in their five-hundred-square-foot apartment, they were within easy walking distance of many pubs, restaurants, and shops. They made the best use of common grounds when entertaining large groups of friends and family, and they became known as the friendliest couple in their apartment building—not only by neighbors but also by maintenance people, the night concierge, and cleaning ladies. "Once, I needed to get into the building through a back door that was locked. A maintenance man let me in the back door, because he knew us."

Later, when they needed to move for the sake of Nick's studies for his MBA at the University of Virginia's Darden Business School, they found a lovely townhouse where every back porch opens onto an enormous green space where dogs and children can romp. They specifically searched out an area that was known for its neighborly atmosphere. The large field and row of back porches allow neighbors to gather around a grill or a fire pit, creating and nurturing social bonds. "Nick and I are both extroverts," she tells me:

> Whenever we need a dose of human interaction, it's great when we can grab the stroller and walk to the nearby town, grocery store, coffee shop, or even stroll down a nice trail. We often quote a TED Talk by James Howard Kunstler, who discussed the tragedy of the suburbs. He said to find a place worth caring about, it must have "something that is terribly important—it has what's called an active and permeable membrane around the edge." And what he meant was a space that is near restaurants, with people walking in and

out, a place where people want to gather. It's important for our family to live near an active and permeable membrane!

Another important factor is having a space we can host. I mentioned that we do not care about square feet. That's because we learned you do not need a lot of space to host parties! We've found guests do not mind being served buffet-style or eating in a yard. In fact, we invited thirty people over tonight for a homemade pizza party. When people ask what they can bring we say BYOC — bring your own chair!

We remind ourselves often that a house is just a house unless you can make it a home through community — through dinners with family members and friends, taking a nice walk outside to greet the neighbors, or walking to the nearby church. The silo effect, separating work from home, neighbors from other neighbors, became even more pronounced during the COVID pandemic, when children could not play with other children (unless they were part of their "bubble"), when neighbors out walking gave other neighbors six feet of space and avoided eye contact, when we weren't even allowed to attend Mass in person, and when many fearful people simply holed up in their own homes for months with no real life human contact.

When we downsized, I had to part with one of my prized possessions, a beautiful Amish cherry farmhouse table. Many Thanksgiving and Christmas dinners and birthday celebrations took place around this table. But now it just can't fit in the dining room. I briefly stored it, disassembled, under our bed. This seemed like a travesty, so I gave it to our son and daughter-in-law who needed a dining room set for their growing family.

I complained to a new neighbor that I didn't know how I was going to be able to have people over for dinner — no room and now, no table! She said we just have to be more creative: sometimes we meet our friends at a local restaurant or pizza place, sometimes we sit outside, sometimes we use a space in the community center. And there's nothing wrong with holding a plate of food on your lap as you sit on the couch!

Our dear friends from college gave their own home to their oldest son and his growing family—while Peter and Robin and the rest of their children moved in with his aging stepfather, who was in need of some extra assistance. It was pretty crowded now in Dad's home, and he fussed a bit about all the new clutter and noise. But having his grandchildren surround him with life and laughter and love was worth every bit of the sacrifice. And nobody regrets spending more time with loved ones as they enter their final years of life.

Let's not lose sight of our primary motivation: growing closer to Our Lord, leaving aside those attachments that threaten to choke off the love of Jesus in our hearts, and loving our neighbor out of love for God.

A frightening event recently shook us to the core and reminded us of the fragility of life, the necessity of daily prayer, and the importance of community—and that we depend for our very existence every moment on the grace of God.

We were in Charlottesville visiting our daughter and son-in-law and their family this past Lent for Nick's birthday, and we were notified early Sunday morning by a string of texts from unidentified numbers that their house had burned down. The family had barely escaped! The fire had turned into a raging inferno even before the smoke detectors had sounded the alarm. Our son-in-law had inexplicably and uncharacteristically woken up and gone downstairs to find a wall of flames in the kitchen. He rushed back upstairs and grabbed the sleeping toddler while our daughter held the baby, and they ran out the front door in bare feet and pajamas. Their community immediately responded, opening their homes and bringing over donations of food, clothing, baby paraphernalia, toys, and shoes! Because they were surrounded by not only their faith community, but also fellow MBA students, the coordination of both spiritual and material necessities was immediately implemented. In the very first few hours after the fire, a receiving house was set up, accompanied by donations and offers to help—all recorded on Excel spreadsheets!

Their love for their community, the life that they had lived for the past two years with its emphasis on hospitality and openness to community, and their own generosity toward neighbors and friends was all returned a hundredfold.

And, in the end, as St. Thérèse reminds us, "all is fleeting that we cherish here under the sun."[56]

Wisdom of St. Thérèse

"You see, Mother, that I am a *very little* soul who can only offer *very little* things to God" writes St. Thérèse. Some of the most beautiful and profound passages in her autobiography are those in which she relates the very simple, humble, often unnoticed acts of charity she performed—often at great cost to her own psyche. She writes, "As you can see, dear Mother, being charitable has not always been so pleasant for me."[57] Yet these simple acts form a constellation of heavenly jewels that are part of the Little Way. Her Little Way gives all of us hope! We, too, in our homes and in our daily lives, can practice simple works of charity as long as we are alert to these opportunities.

During Evening Meditation in the chapel, Thérèse found herself frequently seated near a sister who was constantly fidgeting with a

---

[56] *Story of a Soul*, 50.
[57] *Story of a Soul*, 142.

rosary or some other object. The sound was intensely irritating to Thérèse, who had sensitive ears. She wanted to glare at the nun, but instead she endured it patiently—and even joyfully! By the end of their meditation time, Thérèse would be soaked in sweat from the intensity of this effort! Yet, with characteristic good humor, she writes, "I strove to listen to it carefully as if it were a first-class concert."[58]

There was one nun who particularly irritated Thérèse. Whenever she was tempted to argue with that nun, Thérèse instead would change the subject gently and offer many silent prayers and sacrifices for her. Instead of avoiding her, she went out of her way to do special things for her—always with a sweet smile. One day the nun asked her, "Sister Thérèse, will you please tell me what attracts you so much to me?"[59]

One of my favorite examples of her practice of delicate charity is when Thérèse found herself deeply annoyed by a sister who always splashed dirty water on her as they were washing linens. She decided to accept this irritation cheerfully without wiping her face or letting the other sister know about her distaste; she was grateful for these "treasures" as a way of showing her love to God. Thérèse charmingly adds that she even took a liking to this unusual sacrifice and "decided to turn up as often as I could to that lucky spot where so much spiritual wealth was freely handed out."[60] This simple example shows us that there are infinite ways we can show our love for God and our neighbor and that no suffering needs go to waste.

Thérèse had such a huge heart for Jesus that she wanted to do even more than she already was doing as a Carmelite. She wrote

[58] *Story of a Soul*, 142.
[59] *Story of a Soul*, 127.
[60] *Story of a Soul*, 143.

that she wanted to be a "a warrior, a priest, an apostle, a doctor of the Church, a martyr."[61] In her wisdom, she discovered that all these beautiful and noble desires "are nothing without LOVE. That charity is the EXCELLENT WAY that leads most surely to God.... Then, in the excess of my delirious joy, I cried out: O, Jesus my love ... my *vocation*, at last I have found it ... MY VOCATION IS LOVE!"[62]

St. Thérèse practiced the most exquisite and delicate charity toward her fellow Carmelites out of her profound love for God. "God has allowed me to explore the hidden depths of charity,"[63] she wrote. Even during her final months in the infirmary when she was experiencing the most debilitating spiritual darkness and physical pain, she was always cheerful, joyful, and encouraging toward her sisters. In her last words to Mother Marie de Gonzague: "Everything I have written about my desire for suffering is true!" and "I do not regret having surrendered myself to Love!"[64]

Tip   From the Organizer

House "like things together" and label everything! Coffee supplies should be stored close to the coffee maker, knives close to your prep space, pots and pans close to the stove, etc. When your space is clearly labeled, anyone can come in and put dishes away!

—Jacquelyn Dupuy

---

[61] *Story of a Soul*, 153.
[62] *Story of a Soul*, 181–182.
[63] *Story of a Soul*, 129.
[64] *Story of a Soul*, 248.

Cultivating the Rose of Charity

1. What are some ways we can follow the example of St. Thérèse at home, at work, and in the neighborhood? Can we strive to always have a joyful, calm spirit in the home—even when the kids are sick, grumpy, or moody? We can be cheerful and optimistic and welcoming when a neighbor drops by. We can gladly take on an extra assignment when a co-worker is swamped, and we can smile at the cashier.

2. What are some of the very small opportunities we often overlook—small ways we can show our love for Christ? We can imitate St. Thérèse and offer our sweetest smile to the most irritating person at work, at home, or in our neighborhood.

3. Do we find that there are things that get in the way of fulfilling our obligation to love God with all our heart, mind, and strength? What other things occupy our attention and distract us?

4. Do we reflect on the hunger and extreme poverty that millions of people endure in other parts of the world—and seriously consider what we might personally do to help?

7

The Tranquility of Order

The Rose of Peace

"(He is God!),
who formed the earth and made it
(he established it;
he did not create it a chaos,
he formed it to be inhabited!)."

—Isaiah 45:18

And still peace, always peace,
reigned at the bottom of the chalice.

—St. Thérèse of Lisieux, *Story of a Soul*, 159

In the beginning when the earth was a "formless void," waters covered the earth—the swirling, churning, black waters of primordial chaos. When the ancients spoke of God creating the heavens and the earth, they understood that not only was God the Creator of all things out of nothing, but also He created an essential order, order out of chaos, with everything in a proper relationship with each other and with God.

When God created light and separated it from the darkness, He "called the light Day, and the darkness he called Night" (Gen. 1:5). God creates, and then names, Heaven and earth. Finally on the sixth day, God creates man in His image and likeness. Adam continues the work of God, naming all the creatures of the earth (Gen. 2:19). So Adam is in a sense "imaging" God in his naming of creatures and ordering them. We, too, participate in God's creative powers when we put things in order and put them in proper relationship. Think of cleaning your room as rescuing it from the nonexistence of chaos, a creative endeavor with an element of the divine! Isn't that an intriguing thought? In ordering our own spaces properly, we are actually engaging in a Godly endeavor!

As I take note of my workspace at this moment, I find it cluttered with half a mug of coffee, laptop, pens, scraps of paper, piles of books, unopened mail, a bit of wrapping paper, *Runner's World* magazine, scissors, a random utensil, an iPhone, and a pad of Post-It notes. I feel distracted, uneasy. There's actually a neuroscientific reason for this anxiety! When the eye sees clutter around, the mind sees a problem to be solved ("Where does everything go?"). Our amygdala immediately goes into fight-or-flight mode, causing anxiety. But when the space is clear and tidy and contains only the necessary tools, we feel more focused and sharper. Now, we can attend to the project or task at hand. A proper order (to the space, in our minds) helps us maintain productivity and peace. As Jacquelyn Dupuy says, we should house "like things together" – "Coffee supplies should be stored close to the coffee maker, knives close to your prep space, pots and pans close to the stove, etc."

It's often easier said than done. When you have small children, you barely manage to tidy one space, only to find another being trashed. You finish the morning dishes, only to find your older kids have decided it's time for second breakfast. Meanwhile, the toddler has dumped an entire box of Cheerios on the kitchen floor. Tidying and putting things away seem to be Sisyphean tasks.

When our kids were still very young and we were homeschooling, I would feel mortified if anyone stopped by and saw the house in a mess. School books, worksheets, pencils, and crayons strewn about, breakfast and lunch remains still on the kitchen table, and me still in my sweatpants. I would compare myself to a neighbor mom, who was home baking bread and tidying the house while her kids were at school. When my son's friend came home from school, they would hang out in his friend Steve's perfectly ordered kitchen and eat his mom's freshly baked bread. But upon reflection, I would realize that our households were quite different and that comparisons like this were never fruitful. Furthermore, imparting a proper sense of order to our children doesn't necessarily require an immaculate kitchen, vacuum streaks on the carpet, or food made from scratch.

Keeping things in order is actually a valuable lesson for families. Small children can learn to put things back and keep their toys organized. In fact, toddlers and young children genuinely like to be involved in what they perceive as very important, grown-up work, such as setting the table, putting dishes in the dishwasher, helping cook, and other simple household tasks. If there are bins or baskets they can put their toys in, it becomes even easier. Maria Montessori showed that by having a properly prepared environment, with clear structure and order, children would become calm, peaceful, and capable of learning. This is all the more remarkable because Maria Montessori developed her educational theory while working with children with disabilities and children in the slums of Rome who were struggling with chaos and disorder as they were running wild in the streets.

Keeping our home orderly helps our children learn to be orderly, to use their things properly, and to prepare their minds for learning. And it provides them with security and stability: knowing where things belong, having clean clothes and timely meals, and feeling protected from chaos. But it doesn't have to be obsessive! Clean clothing, bins to put toys in, and healthy meals at regular times all contribute to a sense of order and peace in the home. Order shouldn't take precedence over loving our little ones and allowing for creative spontaneity. We don't have to hold these things in opposition.

Children will learn to respect the property of other family members and grow in a sense of responsibility to the family by putting things back where they belong. It also gives them the first step in learning to order their own thoughts and minds and to begin to grow in virtue. Children will learn to use things properly, to follow appropriate rules, to think logically, to understand principles, and to make reasonable choices.

The Little Way of Living with Less

As parents, we need to exercise prudence as we seek order in our home so that we are not obsessively demanding perfect tidiness or cleanliness when it is not necessary. When the five-year-old excitedly runs into the house carrying flowers he picked for Mom, should we yell at him because he forgot to wipe his feet before entering our clean home? We don't need to reprimand them when they create a messy art project on our kitchen table. We shouldn't be so vain about the state of neatness in our home that we can't even allow a friend to drop by unexpectedly. Order shouldn't be a higher value than loving our family and friends, encouraging their growth, and being able to welcome spontaneity. Order (combined with prudence) instead helps us give our family the best—whether in teaching our kids, providing a peaceful and welcoming environment, or serving others lovingly. Order helps our children feel safe, secure, and loved.

Everything has a place where it belongs. This may include the trash or recycle bin! Everything in the junk drawer actually has a place. The screwdriver goes in the toolbox and the photos in the photo album. The mail needs to be sorted into junk mail and bills, which have their place in a desk rather than on top of the dining room table or the kitchen counter. Everything should be taken out of the drawer or the closet or whatever space you are focusing on, and then each piece is to be analyzed: keep it, throw it away, or donate it. Then each thing must be put away where it belongs.

Start with the junk drawer. If you are one of the few people who doesn't have a junk drawer, you may have another trouble spot you can address—perhaps the infamous "hot spot" where miscellany gathers or an overflowing pantry. Empty it completely. Take everything out and throw away the random crayons, the loose staples, the used tickets, the isolated Band-Aid, the extra picture hooks, the swim team ribbons, and the old Christmas cards. Put the tools in the toolbox, the staples and pens in the desk, the dead iPhones (you know you have them) in the donate bin, and the school photos in the photo album. Reward yourself by using this (now empty) drawer to put away cooking utensils that were taking up valuable space on your kitchen countertop!

When everyone knows where things belong, it is easier to tidy up. When our kids were very young, I labeled the drawers in their rooms so they would know which drawer contained socks, shirts, pants, and so on. Label the *inside* of the kitchen cabinets so your kids can help empty the dishwasher and put things away—while not marring the elegant appearance of the cupboards. One mom suggests that each child pick up five or ten things whenever transitioning to a new activity. Art used to set a kitchen timer and make a game of how many things you can pick up before the timer goes off in three minutes. (The kitchen timer was also invaluable when two small children were fighting over a single toy. The timer became the objective bystander that allowed each child only five minutes to play with the disputed toy before transferring it to the next child.)

The philosopher Fabrice Hadjaj writes in his beautiful book *The Resurrection*:

> The first thing the Risen Lord did was to fold and carefully arrange his face-cloth like a napkin after dinner.... Hence that pervasive sweetness in a home: when the laundry is in its place, when the parquet floor shines, when the table is set, and the aroma from the simmering dish tickles your nostrils, when your clothes are clean.... Isn't this a perfect imitation of God, who formed the earth and made it; he established it; he did not create it a chaos, he formed it to be inhabited (Is 45:18)?[65]

---

[65] Fabrice Hadjadj, *The Resurrection: Experience Life in the Risen Christ* (Paris: Magnificat, 2016), 67–68.

The Little Way of Living with Less

Don't you sometimes wonder why the little detail of folding the face cloth is mentioned at all? After all, Jesus had just risen from the dead! There was an earthquake, an angel has removed the stone, and Jesus is about to appear to His disciples. Yet He takes the time to fold the face cloth and carefully place it apart from the linen cloth. This lovely, simple act seems to speak of His tenderness for humanity, a small gesture of His extravagant love and graciousness.

The Greek theologian and philosopher Christos Yannaras explains that human beings, by nature social animals, cohabitate in a way completely unique from all other animals. Animals may travel in herds or packs or pods and may be territorial over a certain area. Some (like beavers or bees) build dwellings that are protective from predators and feed and allow for propagation. Only human beings create settlements. What differentiates the social cohabitation of human beings from the herd co-existence is the *oikismos*, the settlement, an organization of space around a sacred sign. This sacred sign is the center of the world, even if it changes location because the society is nomadic.[66]

By the same token, don't we have a center of our home—whether it is a physical or observable one? And, if we don't intentionally have a center, what becomes the center? A home may be "well-decorated" or even beautifully appointed without reflecting the truly proper order that we strive for as Catholics. Do we have a crucifix, perhaps, or a cozy family room set apart for playing games with the family or reading quietly, with warm embers crackling in the fireplace? Or do we enthrone the ubiquitous screen with its unnatural glow and electronic pixels in our home?

---

[66] Christos Yannaras, *The Schism in Philosophy* (Brookline: Holy Cross Orthodox Press, 2015), 3. In fact, he says *the presupposition of life itself* is the order and harmony of beauty.

Did you know that Chip and Joanna Gaines of the famed HGTV show *Fixer Upper* have never put a TV in any of their renovations? Joanna explained that when she and Chip were newlyweds, an older couple counseled them to spend their first few weeks of marriage without a TV so that they could focus on each other and spend time doing activities they both loved together. They found they didn't miss the TV at all and simply never bought one. It gave them plenty of opportunities to share dreams, discuss creative goals, and spend quality time together.[67]

Of course, simply having a crucifix or an image of the Sacred Heart or a statue of Mary does not miraculously confer that sense of order that we are striving for as Christian families—from hearts that are centered on God. It certainly helps, though! And every day we can recommit ourselves to order our every activity to the glory of God and to the love and service of our family and neighbors. This internal centering can be renewed each day as we spend time in prayer and reflection on God's Word.

Without a center, we may be constantly chasing after every whim, subject to the vagaries and misconceptions of secular culture or failing to protect our families from the gathering darkness of meaninglessness. In the words of William Butler Yeats, "Things fall apart; the centre cannot hold; Mere anarchy is loosed upon the world."[68]

We may not have a physical shrine in our home, but we can be intentional about our center in many other ways—as many ways as there are unique families! We may consecrate our family to the Sacred Heart of Jesus, have our house blessed, display a crucifix

---

[67] Chip and Joanna Gaines, *The Magnolia Story* (Nashville: W Publishing, 2016), 61-62.

[68] Yeats, "The Second Coming," *The Dial*, 1920.

and other sacred images, and have a designated area of prayer or a special chair where we read Scripture or daily devotions. There are many ways to be intentional about *Who* is the center of our homes. We are a Christian family. God is center. We practice our Catholic Faith. We honor the Blessed Mother and the saints. We try daily to grow in our love for each other and for God.

Many families inadvertently make the center of their home their kids' toys. It is so easy for the toys to pile up, as parents, aunts, uncles, and grandparents shower more presents on birthdays, special occasions, and Christmas. As we welcome more children into our family, we parents want to provide tools for learning and playing. Even well-intentioned parents who vow to purchase only educational toys can see their house slowly turning into a toy store or day care and, in desperation, they hold a garage sale ... until the accumulation begins again!

Despite the fact that the young van Schaijiks had plenty of space in their rented townhouse, they resisted the strong temptation to have a million toys and baby and toddler equipment underfoot. They explain:

> We want to fully welcome our kids into our lives and let them watch and participate as they grow. I think this is very different than letting our lives completely revolve around the kids. We think that the more toys you have, the more the toys become devalued. Furthermore, we want to encourage our kids to love the outdoors and exploring, and if they have every toy they could possibly want, they may not develop their imaginations and a healthy curiosity about the larger world.

This is the order we ultimately strive for: a well-ordered home. Here, "order" means in the first place the proper order of our lives:

with God, with ourselves, and with others. With the proper order, we will find and create peace in our homes. We can take for our model the Holy Family: Fr. Francis Fernandez, author of the *In Conversation with God* series, writes, "The tranquil order of their family life would have created an atmosphere in which Jesus and Joseph could find rest after a full day's work."[69]

Pope Emeritus Benedict XVI discussed in one of his Wednesday audiences how our homes can become centered on Christ: "Every home can transform itself in a little church. Not only in the sense that in them must reign the typical Christian love made of altruism and of reciprocal care, but still more in the sense that the whole of family life, based on faith, is called to revolve around the singular lordship of Jesus Christ."[70]

Wisdom of St. Thérèse

The final words written by Thérèse were, "I go to Him with confidence and love." She throws herself into the arms of Jesus, with complete trust and abandon—just as she had lived her entire life. A hallmark of her Little Way is the peace that enters a soul when completely abandoning itself to the will of God. Even though she made "very little" sacrifices (as she put it)—and even though she herself was "very little"—she had complete confidence in God.

"Today my only guide is self-abandonment. I have no other compass. I no longer know how to ask passionately for anything except that the will of God shall be perfectly accomplished in my soul."[71] Her compass, her guiding light, is nothing other than

---

[69] Francis Fernandez, *In Conversation with God: Meditations for Each Day of the Year* (London: Scepter Press, 1993), vol. 7, 358.
[70] Benedict XVI, Wednesday Audience, February 7, 2007.
[71] *Story of a Soul*, 109.

The Little Way of Living with Less

God's loving will: "It was rather the calm and serene peace of the navigator perceiving the beacon which must lead him to port ... O luminous Beacon of love, I know how to reach You!"[72]

Her Little Way of trust and love offers not only a guiding star but, most importantly, true peace: "How sweet is the way of *love* ... it leaves nothing but a humble and profound peace in the depths of the heart."[73] Even then, in her profound humility, she does not take credit for anything: "To love You as you love me, I must borrow Your love—only then can I have peace."[74] Just one month before she died on September 30, 1897, she was taken outside for the last time to the cloister walk in her bed, and her sister Sr. Genevieve took a photo of her. Emaciated, she tried valiantly to smile as she "unpetaled" a rose over her crucifix. "Exteriorly I am surrounded with flowers; but interiorly I am always in my trial; however, I am at peace!"[75]

Tip   From the Organizer

Work on one space at a time. Feeling like you have to deal with entire categories (all the books in your house, all your clothes, etc.) can tend to overwhelm people. Focusing on one defined space at a time is much more manageable.

—Jacquelyn Dupuy

[72] *Story of a Soul*, 182.
[73] *Story of a Soul*, 170.
[74] *Story of a Soul*, 147.
[75] *Story of a Soul*, 246.

Cultivating the Rose of Peace

1. How can we practice the virtue of orderliness in our lives? How do we set priorities? Do we first submit everything to prayer and ask God to help us rightly order our affairs? What is truly the "center" of our life: ourselves or God?

2. Are our motives pure? That is, do we keep an ordered home so that our family will have peace, a secure and serene life, and a place of repose? Or are we overly focused on "perfection"—to the exclusion of charity? On the other hand, do we avoid excess—the excess of too many toys, clothes, electronics, and other material possessions?

3. How can we implement Pope Emeritus Benedict XVI's beautiful suggestion that our homes be centered on altruism, reciprocal care, and, most importantly, on the Lord Jesus Christ?

4. Can we put aside just a few minutes out of our busy day to make a short visit to the Blessed Sacrament? With this small act of piety, we may find our strength and peace renewed.

8

'Tis the Gift to Be Simple

The Rose of Simplicity

The Lord preserves the simple.

—Psalm 116:6

*Because your soul is extremely simple, but when you
will be perfect, you will be even more simple; the closer
one approaches to God, the simpler one becomes.*

—St. Thérèse of Lisieux, *Story of a Soul*, 148,
quoting subprioress Sr. Febroni

Any discussion of minimalism or downsizing in the home would not be complete without a discussion of simplicity. There is a quote floating around the Internet that is falsely attributed to Leonardo da Vinci: "The height of sophistication is simplicity." In fact, it was said by Clare Boothe Luce, one of America's most famous converts to Catholicism.

One can find sophistication in simplicity, but there is much more depth (and, paradoxically, complexity) to the concept. Simplicity is usually understood as a quality or a thing that is plain, natural, or easy to understand. It can be seen as a concept to be applied to one's home decor, one's style, and oneself—and, as the Amish might use it, as a virtuous way of life.

The author Sue Bender has two degrees, one from Harvard and one from Berkeley. An accomplished artist and therapist, she valued success, achievement, results, and being (in her words) "special." Despite her many accomplishments, however, in her daily life she was frantic and stressed out, with a million things on her daily to do list—never questioning which ones (if any) were truly important. One day she saw Amish quilts hanging in a department store in New York, and she couldn't get them out of her mind: the pattern, the colors, the shapes. Every day she returned to the store to admire the quilts. Her fascination with the makers intensified when she discovered that the Amish also made dolls that have no faces (no eyes, nose, or mouth). The simplicity, yet undeniable beauty, of the quilt and the mysterious faceless dolls captivated a woman whose own life was complicated, frenetic, and intent upon making an impact on the world of high culture.

She purchased her first two faceless dolls from a young Amish midwife named Sarah. She describes visiting the home Sarah lived in to buy the dolls: an immaculate kitchen with a polished woodstove, a table with ten chairs around it, a sparkling-clean living room with a sofa and two straight-backed chairs, and "a lot of empty space."

Bender loved the quilts and the dolls (and that immaculate kitchen) so much that she wanted to live with the Amish in order to better understand why these things drew her. After jumping through many hoops, she was able to find a family that would take her in. She describes the home she is to live in for a summer, as she first walks in: "The room glowed. The feeling went beyond everyday cleanliness and order. The air felt alive, almost vibrating. Can a room have a heartbeat? Can space be serene and exciting at the same time?"[76]

After living with the Amish family and helping out with their daily work, she began to slow down and experience a kind of meditative state of calmness. She learned that every task was done with the same sort of calm; whether canning peas or doing the dishes, each task was done with full attention and care as if it were the most important thing in the world at that moment. They weren't at war with time, as Bender usually was. Rather, "time was full and generous." "No distinction was made between the sacred and the every day," she explains.[77] Their work was important, yet ordinary.

[76] Sue Bender, *Plain and Simple: A Journey to the Amish* (New York: Harper Collins, 2007), ebook, 40.

[77] Bender, *Plain and Simple*, 49.

They didn't work to have free time on the weekend or money for a vacation. Working was being close to God. They were content.

This simplicity and peace that the author so wished to bring into her own life required new attitudes: a humble acceptance of self that is neither self-conscious nor self-aggrandizing but rather is focused on the work itself. She learned to value both the process *and* the product, to live in the present moment (rather than always being in a rush to get somewhere else), to celebrate the ordinary, and to embrace home and community.

Let's imagine how we might incorporate this kind of "Amish" simplicity in our homes: taking time to thoughtfully prepare a meal or bake the bread, focusing on what is most important to achieve the best loaf without unnecessary drama, carefully cleaning everything as we go rather than leaving dishes piled in the sink, and always retaining an attitude of service. To this end, our kitchen will have only what is necessary—clean counter space, bowls, staples, and no "stuff" other than what pertains to the mission. By practicing cleanliness, simplicity, and order, we are better able to serve others rather than simply focusing on pleasing ourselves. By remaining attentive to the present moment, we are better able to discern what God is asking of us, right now.

Simplicity is one of the attributes of God Himself. In fact, theologians say all the other perfections of the divine nature flow from divine simplicity. Whether Jewish, Islamic, or Christian theology, the doctrine of divine simplicity is fundamental. If God is the source and foundation of all things, then God Himself must not be formed of parts (which would then depend on something else in order to come into existence). God is necessary, necessarily existing, and Being itself.

Jesus Christ was perfectly simple as well. In a sermon preached on the feast day of the Little Flower, Msgr. Ronald Knox explores what simplicity means and why we should emulate Jesus and the saints (especially St. Thérèse) who possess this divine quality. Jesus was perfectly simple, says Knox, because He was perfectly integrated. His face was set toward Jerusalem.[78] He didn't look back; He "wasn't looking to see what people were thinking about him, looking to see where his own advantage lay, looking to see what was the best opportunity for striking an impressive attitude or coining a memorable phrase. No, his face was set towards Jerusalem."[79] Jesus was completely focused on fulfilling the will of the Father: "Jesus said to them, 'Truly, truly, I say to you, the Son can do nothing of his own accord, but only what he sees the Father doing; for whatever he does, that the Son does likewise'" (John 5:19). He is truth itself.

If we are simple, Msgr. Knox tells us, we will be integrated. If we are not, we will pick up different points of view, different ideas, or postures or poses, and adopt different styles. We will either believe what everyone else believes or we will be oppositional to what everyone believes. We will want to present an image in order to be liked, to be impressive, or simply to fit in. But the point, says Msgr. Knox, is to be *yourself*—to be truthful, integrated, one with your purpose. To be simple is also to see things with the eyes of God, to distinguish between what is important, what is essential, and what is not—and to be unified within ourselves.

It is certainly no tragedy if our home decor is not stylistically integrated. However, if we ourselves are not integrated, if we fluctuate with every whim, like a weather vane turning in the wind, then we may suffer more serious consequences. If we never think deeply about why we vote a particular way, or how we want to raise

---

78 Ronald Knox, *Pastoral Sermons and Occasional Sermons* (San Francisco: Ignatius Press, 2002), 714.
79 Knox, *Pastoral Sermons*, 714.

our children, or what we value most in life, then we might easily be swayed by everyone else's opinions. It is easy to fall into the trap of being overly concerned with appearances and concerned about what others think, especially when we spend so much time on social media. We compare ourselves or our homes to others who seem to have everything organized, beautiful, and under control. But our concern for appearances can prevent us from growing in holy simplicity. Our concern with appearances or with wanting to impress others may cause us to be less than truthful. We may try to present an image of ourselves or our lives that is "perfect" or that is designed to gain us admiration. We see the negative impact of this on the many Instagrammers who seem to live for generating followers, whether it is through their "perfect" home or life, through histrionics and dramatics, or even through revealing *too much* to total strangers. Once we begin presenting ourselves for the sake of appearances to please different people—behaving in one way at work, another at home, yet another at church, and another for our online presence—we start to become dis-integrated, disingenuous, fractured, and confused in the multitudes of postures we have adopted. Simplicity requires being truthful with ourselves, with others, and with God. Msgr. Knox continues:

> The less we cling to worldly enjoyments, the better chance we shall have of cultivating that true simplicity which is the simplicity of the saints ... the more we can resist the tyranny of these worldly embarrassments, the more we can be content to live according to our income, to be wise according to our opportunities, to be ourselves, to laugh at shams and see things as they are.[80]

---

[80] Knox, *Pastoral Sermons*, 721.

The Little Way of Living with Less

The cardinal virtue of prudence actually guides our practice of the virtue of simplicity because we are not required to let everyone know what is in our hearts. While we ought to be simple and open with God, our family, and dear friends, modesty would, in fact, require that we not over-share intimate things with our co-workers or strangers.

When we approach everything with the purpose in mind, the end goal—like St. Thérèse did, with her single-minded focus on loving God's perfect will—we actually become more free, more integrated, more uniquely ourselves. In fact, when we think about the simplicity of the Amish, with their emphasis on giving God all the glory and on serving others humbly, we can see this as being nearly totally focused on others, rather than self. It is, indeed, to be selfless. As the old Shaker song goes, "When true simplicity is gained, / To bow and to bend we shan't be ashamed." To be focused on the giving, rather than the self, is to be free and simple.

What would integration, simplicity, and openness in our home mean? How might we incorporate holy truthfulness in our decor? It's more than matching colors. It's more than having a specific aesthetic, even, such as "mid-century modern" or "farmhouse style." I would like to suggest that simplicity is an integration of one's family goals or main purpose, or *gestalt*, with their living space. We might ask, "How does the functioning of our home enable us to achieve our ideals as a family? How does our home help us serve our family and our neighbors and strengthen our loving bonds?"

A family that has many children, all of whom are athletes, with multiple practices and games on the schedule, will need to have a home design that offers storage for and accessibility to athletic equipment, shoes, bags, balls, uniforms, towels, and multiple tramping and possibly muddy feet. This home will likely have an entryway or back door (perhaps a mudroom) much different from an elderly couple's retirement home. When my dad returned from the hospital after having broken his hip, we needed to make clear pathways for his walker, removing all throw rugs, furniture, and electrical cords that might impede movement.

Most importantly, however, a family that is striving for sanctity, striving to grow in love with the Lord and with each other, will set their standard to reflect this. The home of a devout Christian family will reflect their love for Jesus. No matter the size of the home, it will have a warm and welcoming feel. When the kids are playing, the toys may be scattered everywhere, of course. But even the most modest home will have a drawer, a basket, or a nook where toys can be put away when play time is over. The home itself is probably not designed to be "impressive" but rather welcoming, peaceful, harmonious. They may have a crucifix in a prominent place; paintings or pictures representing Mary, the saints they admire, and moments from Christ's life; perhaps a statue of St. Francis or St. Fiacre in the garden—but not in an obnoxious or ostentatious or "virtue-signaling" way. That would be the opposite of simplicity! The home would be a natural extension of their peaceful, happy, and harmonious family life.

In the van Schaijik home, simplicity is revealed in their primary focus on being able to have friends and family over for meals and conversations. "We try to remind ourselves often that a house is just a house unless you can make it a home through community—through dinners with family members and friends and taking a nice walk outside to greet the neighbors or walking to the nearby church," they tell me. "These are ways to make a space, even a five-hundred-square-foot space, very special." But the most important thing, as Christ Himself told us, is that our foundation is the secure bedrock of our love for God and, out of love for Him, for our neighbor.

Wisdom of St. Thérèse

Along with humility, simplicity is a key to the spirituality of the Little Way. St. Thérèse admitted that she was a simple soul; she struggled to express herself when she spoke with her spiritual directors—not because she was hiding anything. Her subprioress at the time, Sr. Febronie, laughed about this and reassured Thérèse that this was "because your soul is extremely simple, but when you will be perfect, you will be even more simple; the closer one approaches to God, the simpler one becomes."[81] Her simplicity was part and parcel with her humility!

St. Thérèse wrote that, just as the nature of love is to humble itself, so too does God wish to come into the hearts of the most humble and simple souls. "Our Lord's love is revealed as perfectly in the most simple soul who resists His grace in nothing as in the most excellent soul.... It is to their hearts that God deigns to lower Himself. These are the wild flowers whose simplicity attracts Him."

As Msgr. Knox explains Christ's simplicity as His perfect integration, His focus on the will of the Father, so too was St. Thérèse completely integrated. There was only one thing that mattered to her: love of God. Just as Jesus had "set His face" toward Jerusalem—the Cross—so, too, Thérèse never wavered from her own pursuit of God's will and the love of Jesus Christ: "I made the resolution never to wander far away from the glance of Jesus in order to travel peacefully toward the eternal shore."[82] And soon

---

[81] *Story of a Soul*, 148.
[82] *Story of a Soul*, 64.

she would face the cross herself. "I care now about one thing only—to love You, my Jesus!"[83] Just as Jesus had died in agony on the Cross, so too did Thérèse suffer the agony of suffocating as she died from tuberculosis. Her last words were recorded by Mother Agnes, and among these last words she said, "I do not regret having surrendered myself to Love."[84]

Tip From the Organizer

If you're not in a rush, and see a task can be completed in five minutes or less, do it! Sort your mail over the recycling bin, so you're able to throw out junk mail immediately. Empty the dishwasher. Dust one room. And so on.

—Jacquelyn Dupuy

[83] *Story of a Soul*, 156.
[84] *Story of a Soul*, 248.

Cultivating the Rose of Simplicity

1. How can we grow in the virtue of simplicity? Do we tend to exaggerate to make a point? Do we over-share on social media out of vanity? Are we pretentious or falsely humble?

2. Who is at the center of our hearts? Can we make a better effort to put Christ first and foremost as we begin each day, as we begin each activity, and as we end our day? How can we remind ourselves throughout the day to remain focused on doing God's will rather than our own?

3. Do we take the time to think deeply about what our goals and ideals are, about the goals and ideals that motivate us and unify our family? Is our family pro-life? Do we strive to protect the vulnerable and the dignity of all? How can we live this out in our daily lives?

4. When we have conflicting desires, we feel internally divided and anxious. Can we set aside some time to spend in Eucharistic Adoration, asking Christ to give us His peace and to make us whole?

9

Ever Ancient, Ever New

The Rose of Beauty

Out of Zion, the perfection of beauty, God shines forth.

—Psalm 50:2

*I understood how all the flowers He has created are beautiful,
how the splendor of the rose and the whiteness of the lily do
not take away the perfume of the little violet or the delightful
simplicity of the daisy. I understood that if all flowers wanted
to be roses, nature would lose her springtime beauty.*

—St. Thérèse of Lisieux, Story of a Soul, 35

Imagine this scene: we are driving past a shabby neighborhood in an otherwise upscale, charming tourist town. A hand-lettered sign, "free COVID testing," hangs lopsided on a small tent across the street; a few folks are milling about. The brick row houses all look the same, slightly unkempt as though their landlords decided it wasn't worth their time or money to paint trim or repair windows. Fences are sagging, screens are torn, a few windows are blocked by ancient air conditioning units, chugging noisily. A small alleyway draws my attention: back doors facing each other, open onto the grass-lined alley. In the center, rows of colorful laundry flutter in the breeze as they hang neatly on lines. Each clothesline is parallel with their neighbors' laundry, making a bright artwork—a Rothko come to life. It's a surprising spot of beauty in the midst of a space that seemed otherwise mundane and even rundown. It reminds me that we can find beauty almost everywhere, if we are alert to it.

The late, great British philosopher Sir Roger Scruton explains that when you study closely the great landscape painters, you will discover that they were not trying to simply "paint a pretty scene" but were grappling with suffering, death, decay, and the vastness of the universe—and hinting at these themes through subtle techniques. They were able to grasp the beauty that "lies incipient in decay ... the eternal that is implied in the transient."[85]

The charm and beauty of this neighborhood scene rests perhaps in the marriage of many simple things: the potential for the neighbors to gather, their belonging to a community, the order and timeliness of the laundry hanging out, the smell of sun on freshly washed clothes, the superiority of sun-dried laundry. (With a dryer there's no possibility of chatting with the neighbors, no disinfection effect of sunlight.)

Sometimes in our efforts to achieve perfection we can lose sight of the *simple beauties* that are within our reach and that will afford us pleasure in a way that more grandiose efforts do not—and, even worse, may be counterproductive to providing the nurturing and loving home environment we desire. The famous aphorism that "The perfect is the enemy of the good" applies here. When your child is feeling ill, you will turn to a warm slice of buttered cinnamon toast rather than undertaking an elaborate Julia-Child-style beef bourguignon, which is neither timely nor appealing to the invalid. It simply would not be appropriate or fitting to the situation. In the same way, beauty in the home is not meant to be akin to a museum or something to post on Instagram or to impress your neighbors! I've seen many Instagram posts where someone says they will "order some old books" to create a bookshelf that appears vintage or is color-matched. The notion that you would have to buy "fake" books—that is, books you don't actually read but are there simply to make a statement—is absurd. It not only violates the principle of simplicity and truthfulness, but also fails to capture the "quality without a name."

[85] Roger Scruton, *Beauty: A Very Short Introduction* (New York: Oxford University Press, 2011), 146.

Christopher Alexander takes a somewhat socratic approach to his inquiries into what makes a home *home*. What makes a room or a building or a town beautiful, functional, and truly livable? He calls this mysterious quality the "quality without a name." He writes,

> Imagine yourself on a winter afternoon with a pot of tea, a book, reading light, and two or three huge pillows to lean back against.... You put the tea where you can reach it: but in a place where you can't possibly knock it over. You pull the light down, to shine on the book, but not too brightly, and so that you can't see the naked bulb. You put the cushions behind you, and place them, carefully, one by one.[86]

You can almost feel the coziness of that reading nook on a gray afternoon; perhaps snowflakes are just beginning to flutter outside your window while a thick volume awaits your leisure. Alexander goes on to unpack how the "quality without a name" involves an element of "comfort"—yet, not comfort in a superficial sense, which he likens to having too much money, a too-soft bed, or a room that always has an even temperature. The appropriate kind of comfort described here is when the furnishings and surroundings match the activities and events that continually take place in this particular spot; the material things are well-ordered to the purpose of this space. This spot is meant for reading, and every object is perfectly suited to this human endeavor—that is, perfectly suited for the people who actually live in this home.

In our living room, we have a lovely pale-rose, mid-century, modern-style chair from West Elm that I purchased impulsively as a reading chair. It may be "beautiful" in the sense that it has

---

[86] Alexander, *The Timeless Way of Building*, 32.

nice, clean lines and the color really complements the decor. The problem is that nobody sits in it unless every other seat is taken and you are too old to sit on the floor and too tired to continue standing. The lovely chair is not "comfortably" suited (in the good sense of comfort described above) to the activities that take place. It's not good for reading, or for conversing, or for taking a short nap on a cold winter day, curled up in a blanket.

The truly "comfortable" space described by Alexander above is the perfect space for reading on a cold winter morning. The pillows may not be West Elm, but they are cozy and supportive. The light is at the right angle for reading (not just to look "good on the 'Gram"), and a table is within easy reach. And this, too, is part of beauty in the way we are considering it here. A home is beautiful if it is perfectly suited to the family who dwells therein: it is happy, peaceful, secure.

Sir Roger Scruton points out that there are many instances in which the beauty we perceive is not a "masterpiece," a dramatic or supreme beauty, like the Cathedral at Chartres or—in the example he uses—Baldassare Longhena's church on the Grand Canal in Venice, the Church of Santa Maria della Salute. If everything considered beautiful were like that, they would all vie for attention and perhaps might even cancel out our recognition of beauty. The humble beauty of the street that surrounds the Church of Santa Maria della Salute actually contributes in a way to our appreciation of the beauty of the church. Here Sir Roger echoes St. Thérèse's illustration of the varying beauties of the flowers, that if every flower (or soul) were a beautiful rose, there would be no wildflowers with their delicate scents or simple charms. Similarly, our appreciation of the "humble" beauties of our daily lives contributes to our satisfaction with our lives, our gratitude to God for His many gifts, and our aesthetic appreciation of our homes.

"There is an aesthetic minimalism exemplified by laying the table, tidying your room, designing a website, which seems at first sight quite remote from the aesthetic heroism exemplified by Bernini's *St. Teresa in Ecstasy* or Bach's *Well-Tempered Clavier*."[87] Nonetheless, you want your table, the room, or the website "to look right," and this looking-right involves being pleasing to the eye and conveying intended meanings and values. Scruton concludes that we should consider beauty as a form of fittingness or harmony.

When we seek to make our space beautiful, it would seem that in addition to order and fittingness (to our actual space and to our activity within that space), we want a pleasing appearance. Beauty, Scruton tells us, speaks to us of human fulfillment.[88] But human fulfillment in a way it ought to be. So, in our search for a "minimal" beauty in our ordinary lives, in our humble abode, we seek to create a space in which our life, our human activities, can flower and become what they ought to be — not just in the way we want, but in the way we *ought* to want, in a way that is consistent with God's vision for us.

The simplicity and even beauty found in the untrammeled world, in fresh laundry hanging neatly in rows, fluttering in the breeze and sunshine, in the butterflies and puddles found on a walk with a toddler — all this beauty can be found far more frequently in our everyday lives if we are on the lookout for it. My favorite poet, Gerard Manley Hopkins, was a master of finding the beauty "deep down things." He sees God's grace in a candle in a window; the wing of a bird in flight; furrows of freshly plowed soil; the stippling on a trout. "The world is charged with the grandeur of God,"[89] he sings.

---

87 Scruton, *Beauty*, 8.
88 Scruton, *Beauty*, 123.
89 Hopkins, "God's Grandeur" (1877).

The Little Way of Living with Less

The unique and unrepeatable beauty of individual things was given to us by God and lifts our hearts and minds to the loving Creator.

And, aren't these everyday beauties just what we really appreciate in our daily lives—and what often bring us to an awareness of the presence of God? Scruton reflects: "The beauty of an unpretentious street, a nice pair of shoes or a tasteful piece of wrapping paper ... these minimal beauties are far more important to our daily lives."[90] It's that sense of beauty in our daily surroundings—the window in the dining room that is filled with the fluttering green of the birch tree outside, the painting passed down through the generations from our grandmother, the deep warmth of an old cherrywood hutch, the porch with a swing overlooking a green lawn sparking with fireflies. We need the experience of beauty in our ordinary, daily lives.

Most of us are familiar with Chip and Joanna Gaines, the duo who revitalized the town of Waco, Texas, with their *Fixer Upper* reality television series. Joanna tells the story of how they first began fixing up homes—beginning with their own first little home. With excruciating attention to detail, she had "perfectly" renovated and decorated their first home: "I looked around and saw a lot of 'perfection,' and I thought, *But where do my kids sit? Why don't my kids have a play space of their own anywhere in this house?* She then had a moment of realization: "If all I'm doing is creating beautiful spaces, I'm failing. But if I'm creating beautiful spaces where families are thriving, then I'm really doing something."[91]

This element of fittingness and comfort, appropriateness to the situation and for the purpose of the home—where families can more than simply live, more than simply look good, but *thrive*.

[90] Scruton, *Beauty*, 10.
[91] Gaines and Gaines, *The Magnolia Story*, 119, 130.

Nick and Lucy van Schaijik, who furnish their home with many hand-me-downs and thrifted or Facebook Marketplace finds, explain that they prefer buying used furniture made with real materials and good workmanship, which should last much longer than an inexpensive Wayfair or Ikea product. They believe, "If you want things that will be beautiful for a long time, buy things that have been beautiful for a long time." And, if the furniture in question is a hand-me-down from parents or grandparents, with a history of being loved and cared for, then it is much more than an object to fill a space—it is a "memory to last a lifetime."

A few years ago my daughter and I visited her best friend who was spending time at her parents' home while her husband (a Naval officer) was deployed. We enjoyed the generous hospitality of her parents as we stayed in their childhood home. Though this home was filled with mementos and furnishings of decades of children, one particular collection stood out for me. I woke in the morning to the aroma of freshly brewed coffee. I was invited to make myself at home in the kitchen, so I went to the cupboard to get a coffee mug. As I opened the cupboard, I was greeted by a colorful collection of handmade pottery mugs, each one unique. I realized that not a single one was "standard," chipped, or ugly. Our host laughed. "I wanted to be able to always have the 'best mug,'" she said, "even after everyone else has made their selection!" I resolved right then to throw out or give away all the ugly, non-joy-sparking mugs that cluttered our kitchen cabinets. The same goes for many other household items: we sometimes store many items that have no real beauty or significance and may even be damaged, simply because we have a cabinet for them, even though we may be piling mugs on top of mugs or glassware in front of glassware. When you have fewer items, it will be easier to see what you have, and your shelves will look tidier.

The Little Way of Living with Less

The popular (albeit controversial) Canadian psychologist Jordan Peterson writes in his latest book, *Beyond Order*, that we should try to make at least one thing beautiful and this will help us connect with the divine. Peterson suggests: make one room beautiful.[92] This, we can do. Here we can begin. Don't tackle the entire house at once but, rather, begin with one significant spot: perhaps a corner where you like to pray in the morning; perhaps the kitchen where you show your love for your family by cooking nutritious meals; perhaps the bedroom, where you've decided to make that bed first thing in the morning and leave the space calm and peaceful; or perhaps the guest room, for you've resolved to grow your gift of hospitality and generosity. Maybe you have one beautiful vase that sits in a cabinet unused: fill that vase with some freshly cut flowers and place it in a prominent spot for all to enjoy. St. Josemaría Escrivá in his practical, down-to-earth way tells us, "Begin by making the best use of what you have."[93]

The point is not to have a "perfect" house, to have every room so beautiful that people don't feel comfortable, or even to have everything obsessively tidy so that we have lost the real point of our homemaking. Our primary goal is love: How can we love our family and friends and strengthen the bonds between us through our hospitality, our generosity, our welcoming inclusion? The point is not to indulge in a self-centered obsession over our own homes, our tidiness, or having the most beautiful place. And isn't the most beautiful home not necessarily the one marked by physical

---

[92] Jordan Peterson, *Beyond Order: 12 More Rules for Life* (New York: Penguin/Portfolio, 2021), 201.

[93] Fernandez, quoting St. Josemaría Escrivá, *In Conversation with God*, vol. 2, 391.

beauty but the one with a beauty that springs from order, simplicity, mutual respect, love and service, and peace?

The Greek philosopher Christos Yannaras says that the original meaning of the Greek word for beauty (*kallos*) includes order, harmony, and decorum. God created the cosmos to be a beautiful, orderly system. Yannaras explains that the Greek word *kosmos* more accurately means "ornament" or "adornment" (from which perhaps we get the word cosmetics); reality itself has the character of decorum and beauty. Beauty is "the mode by which beings *are* in their totality."[94] Isn't that a lovely thought: the universe is God's ornament! And when something is fully what it is meant to be, as God designed it to be, it is beautiful. Perhaps this is why the experience of beauty points us beyond this world, where "our immortal longings and our desire for perfection are finally answered."[95] The experience of beauty tells us that, although we feel at home in this world, we are also drawn to another world, the eternal, where our "longings and desire for perfection are answered." *Out of Zion, the perfection of beauty, God shines forth!*

Wisdom of St. Thérèse

Even as a small child, Thérèse was aware of the beauty of creation. She describes the "golden days" of her early childhood, with long walks on Sundays and visits to her father's pavilion. "I can still feel the deep emotion I felt when I saw the fields of wheat starred with poppies, cornflowers, and daisies."[96] The vivid memory of these beautiful wildflowers in the open fields may have helped inspire her to call herself the Little Flower, but it was when meditating

---

[94] Yannaris, *The Schism in Philosophy*, 317.
[95] Scruton, *Beauty*, 145.
[96] *Story of a Soul*, 27.

on a picture that her sister Pauline had given her, "the little flower of the Divine Prisoner," that she offered herself to Jesus as His little flower.[97]

She had her own garden spot where she grew flowers, and she loved going fishing with her father: "I was very fond of the countryside, flowers, birds, etc. Sometimes I would try to fish with my little line, but I preferred to go alone and sit down on the grass bedecked with flowers, and then my thoughts became very profound indeed!"[98] One very sweet memory was when she would scatter flower petals before the Blessed Sacrament when there was a procession on feast days. "I was never so happy as when I saw my roses *touch* the sacred monstrance."[99]

All things point to God; all creation gives Him glory. "Never will I forget the impression the sea made upon me; I couldn't take my eyes off it since its majesty, the roaring of its waves, everything spoke to my soul of God's grandeur and power," wrote St. Thérèse.[100] Thérèse always rejoiced in the beauty of God's creation, even at the end of her life when she was suffering excruciating physical and spiritual pain. She continued to strew flowers before the Lord, both literally and figuratively. In her final days of life when she was brought out of the infirmary into the cloister walk, she "unpetaled" her roses over her crucifix.

Yes, my Beloved, this is how my life will be consumed. I have no other means of proving my love for you other than that of strewing flowers, that is, not allowing one little sacrifice to escape, not one look, one word, profiting by all

[97] *Story of a Soul*, 80.
[98] *Story of a Soul*, 54.
[99] *Story of a Soul*, 33.
[100] *Story of a Soul*, 64.

the smallest things and doing them through love. I desire to suffer for love and even to rejoice through love; and in this way I shall strew flowers before Your throne. I shall not come upon one without *unpetalling* it for You.[101]

Tip | From the Organizer

Make categories for all objects to be sorted into: keep, donate, trash/recycle, store elsewhere. Only keep things that you need (use) or love.

—Jacquelyn Dupuy

[101] *Story of a Soul*, 184.

Cultivating the Rose of Beauty

1. What can we do to add beauty in our homes—the simple beauty of cleanliness, order, and tranquility? We don't need to create a perfectly staged or designer-level beauty; perhaps a simple vase of flowers on the kitchen table or the display of a favorite ceramic pot in a clean kitchen will achieve this.

2. Consecrate our home to the Blessed Mother, so that she may help us to take care of it "as though it were the house of God Himself."

3. Is our home a place of refuge? Do family members feel encouraged and guests feel welcome? Do we strive to make at least one room beautiful each day?

4. St. Teresa of Calcutta often said, "Do something beautiful for God." What are the flowers that we can strew before God's throne in our daily lives?

10

Sun in the Morning

The Rose of Gratitude

Then said Jesus, "Were not ten cleansed?
Where are the nine? Was no one found to return
and give praise to God except this foreigner?"

—Luke 17:17–18

Only in heaven will you understand the
gratitude that overflows my heart.

—St. Thérèse of Lisieux, *Story of a Soul*, 175

What makes us happy? We often think that our life experiences, the circumstances in which we live, cause us to be happy or not. But researchers have found that even when someone wins the lottery, buys a new house, gets married, or otherwise experiences a serendipitous life event, their overall sense of happiness and satisfaction is only briefly impacted, and then they go back to baseline. It turns out that only about 10 percent of our emotional well-being is actually due to life circumstances! Our genetics (including our temperament) and our thoughts, beliefs, and actions actually have the most impact on our sense of happiness and contentment.[102] In short, happiness is an "inside job."

Yet how much of our daily life is spent focusing outward—on what we have or don't have, or on what others have?

A huge temptation (especially for women) is to compare ourselves with our friends, to suffer anxiety about the way we look, the way our homes look, the way our children behave, and to wish our lives were other than they are. We forget that external appearances do not tell the whole story. We fret that the woman who attends daily Mass with all seven of her perfectly behaved children is so much better than we are, much more holy, and that we are failures.

---

[102] Claudia Wallis, "The New Science of Happiness," *Time*, January 17, 2005.

The Little Way of Living with Less

With the advent of social media, especially Instagram and the opportunity it affords to have a glimpse into personal details of other people's homes and lives (a glimpse that could never have happened twenty years ago), we are even more able to make assumptions about other people's lives and to view ourselves as lacking. Where does that woman who sews all her own curtains, cooks everything from scratch, DIYs a home renovation, and also is incredibly fit and beautiful get all that energy and talent?

Do we experience a twinge of dissatisfaction, anxiety, or even sadness every time we scroll through social media? In the wake of the coronavirus pandemic, "Doomscrolling" became a thing. The name is apt. The more we scroll, the less happy we become, especially when we engage in comparing ourselves to those whose lives we see (with filters and editing) on social media. We think: "If only I had a bigger house, or a more fulfilling career, or a high income or ... or ... or ... *Then* I'd be happy."

"Compare and despair," as a priest once told me.

In our First World country with all our comforts and consumerism, combined with the omnipresence of social media, the capital sins of envy and greed may become a threat to our spiritual life—even for those of us who attend Mass daily and consider ourselves spiritually healthy. Every time I scroll through Instagram, purportedly with the intent to catch up with friends I haven't seen in a while or to listen to a Scripture reflection by Bishop Barron, I end up dwelling on photos of newly decorated or updated homes, falling prey to West Elm ads for adorable pillows or a velvet armchair, or checking out a friend's home renovation.

The tiny, twisted seed of envy is planted in my soul, and I feel a twinge of dissatisfaction, a slight feeling of unhappiness with being here, now. If we water that tiny seed with our imagination and allow our desires to roam freely, we nurture the bud of envy. We begin by wishing our lives were different, better, more like our Instagram friends' lives. We allow resentment and mean-spirited thoughts to enter in. We think, "Jane's husband is probably annoyed with the way she is constantly redecorating the dining room." There must be some secret struggle that darkens our friend's mood and lessens her joy. Soon the small seed grows into the dark fruit of envy.

Envy caused Satan to rebel against God, Cain to murder his brother, and the brothers of Joseph to sell him into slavery. St. Basil the Great, who lived in the fourth century AD, wrote a famous homily on envy that has wisdom that is highly applicable today. "Free yourself entirely from the desire for any kind of earthly riches or from the esteem to be gained from possessing worldly goods. Ownership of these things is not under your control.... Virtue is within our power."[103]

Sometimes it isn't the comparisons we make with others or envy: it is our own internal critic that keeps pushing us, telling us that we are not good enough and causing the anxiety that cripples us and steals our joy and our peace. Our inner critic turns negativity, harshness, and self-loathing upon ourselves: "You will never be successful, you are not worthy, you always fail, you are not lovable." And this inner critic can soon take over like weeds in a garden, poisoning our lives and subverting our happiness.

Joanna Gaines relates that she was constantly pushing herself to do more, to be more perfect, to create a more perfect home. In the midst of some very serious financial challenges, she suddenly realized that it was up to her to change her attitude. She could *choose* to be merely surviving day to day, always frustrated about

---

[103] St. Basil, *The Fathers of the Church: St. Basil*, trans. Sr. M. Monica Wagner, C.S.C. (Washington, DC: Catholic University of America Press, 1962), 473.

cleaning up yet another mess or dirty fingerprint ... or she could choose each day, each moment, to actually *thrive*. She discovered that you can't wait until everything is perfect to thrive. You thrive in the present moment, amid the messiness of life. "If you can't find happiness in the ugliness, you're not going to find it in the beauty, either ... In the end, what it's all about is thankfulness and contentment."[104]

The focus of our attention is not making us happier because we are not focused on what really matters: the one, good thing, as St.Thérèse said.

Spiritual writers and saints have known this for centuries, yet only now contemporary psychologists are catching up with the fact that being grateful makes you feel happier. Dr. Martin Seligman, the founder and leading proponent of positive psychology, studies the "science of happiness." Simple things like being thankful, expressing our gratitude to others, performing acts of kindness, and writing down things we appreciate each day are ways to increase our sense of happiness. We can consciously, intentionally choose to be grateful (no matter the circumstances!) and thereby increase our joy in life. Hearkening back to St. Basil's homily on envy, we see that "Virtue is within our power!"

Not only are happiness and virtue within our power through gratitude, but even more surprisingly, gratitude brings down heavenly graces! When only the one leper out of ten that were healed returned to Jesus to give thanks and to praise God, Jesus asked him, "Were not ten cleansed? Where are the nine?" And then Jesus said, "Rise and go your way; your faith has made you well" (Luke 17:17–19). The fact that Christ adds the blessing, "your faith has made you well" suggests that the Samaritan will receive

---

[104] Gaines and Gaines, *The Magnolia Story*, 167, 168.

even more abundant blessings and graces from God because of his humble gratitude.

As baptized Christians, we are called to share the Good News! How can we share our joy in Christ if we are wallowing in self-pity, always discontented, or failing to be grateful for our blessings? As a warning—and perhaps a way of motivating us to strive to be grateful—Fr. Jacques Philippe explains that if you are *always* sad and discontented, you will actually receive less and less of God's graces! This is a rather shocking reality! He writes:

> If you recognize what you have received, if you are grateful for the good and beautiful things already present in your life, you'll receive still more. But if you are always discontented and dissatisfied, you'll receive less and less. It is not God's fault, nor can you blame the hardness of your life; the problem is that you shut yourself up in your discontent and resentment.[105]

The prophet Jonah successfully warned the great city of Nineveh to repent. His efforts were met with huge success. The king repented in sackcloth and ashes; he also made each of his subjects—including the cattle and sheep!—fast and wear sackcloth and ashes. Yet Jonah became depressed. He was angry that God did not destroy the city. He went off by himself and told God that he wanted to die. God sent a gourd plant to give him shade from the desert sun. His depression lifts momentarily. But when God sends a worm to kill the plant, Jonah again becomes depressed to the point of asking to die, saying "I would be better off dead than alive."

Sometimes we read this account with a bit of puzzled amusement over Jonah, who wants to die because his little gourd plant is gone.

---

[105] Philippe, *The Way of Trust and Love*, 113–114.

God reminds Jonah that people of Nineveh, whom He has spared, are more important than possessions. "And the Lord said, 'You pity the plant, for which you did not labor, nor did you make it grow, which came into being in a night, and perished in a night. And should not I pity Nineveh, that great city, in which there are more than a hundred and twenty thousand persons who do not know their right hand from their left, and also much cattle?" (Jon. 4:10-11).

When we reflect on it a little more, we might realize that Jonah is exhibiting some of the same failings we experience in our daily lives. First, he is angry over God's mercy because Jonah had preached doom and destruction. Even though he was one of the only—maybe *the* only—prophets who were not run out of town, killed, or brutalized for their prophesies, he is not grateful for God's mercy. Second, he becomes attached to a creature that is clearly a gratuitous gift from God. When we reflect on how this sort of ingratitude for, and lack of awareness of, God's mercy plays out in our own lives, we recognize the same "wicked sadness" that steals our joy and vitality. This sadness comes upon us when we become too attached to our own possessions, our own plans, our own selfish desires. The antidote is gratitude.

Once we make it a priority, we can be grateful for so many things! We can especially take notice of those things we take for granted each day—a sunny day, flowers outside our window (so appreciated by St. Thérèse from her infirmary bed), the sound of a mournful train whistle in the distance, the smell of bread baking, a cup of strong coffee, a hot shower, a good friend. Dr. Seligman recommends writing letters of gratitude whenever we can so as to increase in us the joy that comes from this attitude of gratitude.

In fact, we are told many times in Scripture to rejoice. St. Paul writes from his captivity in Rome to the Philippians: "Rejoice in the Lord always; again I will say, Rejoice" (4:4). In Colossians, he urges us that as Christians we should be "abounding in

thanksgiving" (2:7). The apostle tells us as well that the fruit of the
Spirit is love, joy, peace, patience, kindness, generosity, faithfulness,
gentleness, and self-control" (Gal. 5:22-23). If one of the fruits of
the Spirit is joy, then it is certainly possible for us to rejoice always!
We can ask the Holy Spirit to increase in us those beautiful gifts.

When Moses was nearing death, having brought the grumbling,
back-sliding Israelites to the Promised Land after forty years in the
desert, he delivers a final exhortation: "Hear, O Israel: The Lord
is our God, the Lord alone," which is the beginning of the great
Shema prayer, recited every day by the Jews:

> And when the Lord your God brings you into the land
> which he swore to your fathers, to Abraham, to Isaac, and
> to Jacob, to give you, with great and goodly cities, which you
> did not build, and houses full of all good things, which you
> did not fill, and cisterns hewn out, which you did not hew,
> and vineyards and olive trees, which you did not plant, and
> when you eat and are full, then take heed lest you forget
> the Lord, who brought you out of the land of Egypt, out
> of the house of bondage. (Deut. 6:10-12)

Take heed lest you forget the Lord! Are we not all in the same situation
as the Israelites, living in cities we didn't build, using goods we did
not manufacture, with many talents and blessings we did nothing
to merit? Everything is a gift from God! A first-century Jewish writer
explained that the activity most characteristic of God is to give
His blessings. And thanksgiving is therefore the most appropriate
response by Creation.[106] Daily expressing our gratitude and love
toward God helps us keep our focus on what truly matters, helps

[106] Philo, as quoted by Edward Sri, *A Biblical Walk through the Mass*
(West Chester, PA: Ascension Press, 2021), 120.

us appreciate the present moment, inspires confidence and trust in God's love and mercy, and opens ourselves in gratitude to the abundant graces God wishes to shower upon us.

G. K. Chesterton wrote in *Orthodoxy* that the only way to save Pimlico (a part of London he considered to be "desperate") was to love it like the way a mother loves her children: unconditionally, without any reason—simply because they are her children. After all, "Men did not love Rome because she was great. She was great because they had loved her."[107]

This is the same insight that Joanna Gaines had when she decided to thrive instead of survive. She decided to love the dirty fingerprints on her white sofa, the spilled milk, and the art projects on her dining room table. She resolved to be fully present to her family and to be grateful in the moment. And her home and her family began to thrive! So, let's make our homes gracious and welcoming to all and filled with gratitude to God and to our families.

Wisdom of St. Thérèse

Being grateful to God is at the heart of St. Thérèse's "Little Way." She mentions gratitude over and over in her *Story of a Soul* and also in the memoirs of her sister Céline. For example, she writes, "Jesus does not demand great actions from us, but simply surrender and gratitude."[108]

Thérèse writes in such a simple and uplifting way that we might be tempted to think she was naturally optimistic or that it was easy for her to be so cheerful. She writes, "God has given me the grace not to be downcast at any passing thing. When I think of the past,

---

[107] Hat tip to Katie van Schaijik for sharing Thomas Dougherty's favorite quote.

[108] *Story of a Soul*, 176.

my soul overflows with gratitude when I see the favors I received from heaven." [109] Nonetheless, she experienced intense suffering throughout her short life: through her own sensitivity as a young child, the childhood loss of her mother, in the convent through her many silent sacrifices, and then finally through her illness and spiritual dark night. "My heart overflows with gratitude when I think of this inestimable treasure that must cause a holy jealousy to the angels of the heavenly court. My desire for suffering was answered, and yet my attraction for it did not diminish.... [F]rom our hearts came only sighs of love and gratitude!"[110]

Throughout, Thérèse begged for God's graces with complete humility and confidence, expected an abundance of them, and then effusively thanked God for every blessing and every cross. Gratitude has the ability to draw down God's grace! "What most attracts God's graces is gratitude, because if we thank him for a gift, he is touched and hastens to give us ten more, and if we thank him again with the same enthusiasm, what an incalculable multiplication of graces! I have experienced this: try it yourself and you will see!" [111]

One month prior to her death, St. Thérèse felt as though she were suffocating with every breath. Her difficulty breathing, coughing, chest pains, and swollen limbs had finally been diagnosed as tuberculosis. All the while, she was also going through a terrible "underground passage," enduring a dark night of the soul. Nonetheless, she continued to give everyone smiles, advice, and encouragement, and she even joked with them. Despite the pain being like "iron spikes," she told Mother Agnes, "Don't be sad at

---

[109] *Story of a Soul*, 99.

[110] *Story of a Soul*, 152.

[111] Philippe, *The Way of Trust and Love*, 111.

seeing me sick like this, little Mother! You can see how happy God is making me. I am always cheerful and content."[112]

Tip — From the Organizer

It does not matter how you got to your starting point. Where there is breath, there is hope! Make a list of things that need to be tackled, in the order of importance to you. Then, make a list of prayer intentions to offer up for each task. Offer God your work, as a prayer for that intention. For example: I used to offer up washing dishes for the conversion of a friend whose name started with "D."

—Jacquelyn Dupuy

[112] *Story of a Soul,* 243.

Cultivating the Rose of Gratitude

1. Are we grateful each day for the many blessings we receive—for our lives, our families, a safe place to live, water, food, and so on? Each day in our morning and evening prayer, we can remember to praise God and give Him thanks.

2. Do we remember to thank our families for their many gifts and acts of service? Sometimes we take for granted the many things our loved ones do for us: provide for us, cook, clean, pray for us, love us, and so much more. When my husband takes out the garbage, I try to remember to thank him for that. These small gestures of love should not be taken for granted.

3. "Rejoice in the Lord always!" (Phil. 4:4). Do we consciously try to maintain this attitude of joy and inner peace, even when circumstances are troubling or difficult?

11

True Home

Life in the Rose Garden

How lovely is thy dwelling place,
O Lord of hosts!
My soul longs, yea, faints
for the courts of the Lord;
my heart and flesh sing for joy
to the living God.

—Psalm 84:1–2

I imagine I was born in a country that was covered in thick fog. I
never had the experience of contemplating the joyful appearance
of nature flooded and transformed by the brilliance of the sun. It
is true that from childhood I heard people speak of these marvels,
and I know the country I am living in is not really my true
fatherland, and there is another I must long for without ceasing.

—St. Thérèse of Lisieux, *Story of a Soul*, 195

Our fascination with things of the world, our sinking so easily into the comforts of materialism and for settling with appearances, the "dictatorship" of our desires, our attraction to all that glitters (whether material possessions, power, status, or creature comforts) is only countered by the encounter with the living God.

Philosopher Ludwig Wittgenstein (a baptized, though nonpracticing Catholic) wrote in his diaries: "I myself turn my gaze toward worldly things; unless 'God visits me.'"[113]

And God indeed visits us.

God intended for us to be with Him in Paradise; He walked in the Garden of Eden visiting Adam and Eve during the breezy time of the day. But as a result of man's disobedience, we were expelled. Nonetheless, God continued to seek out His people: when the earth was completely filled with violence and God decided to make an end of it, He preserved the righteous Noah and his family; He established His covenant with Abraham and promised to make of him a great nation with descendants as numerous as the stars in Heaven; and He rescued the Israelites from slavery

---

[113] Julian Carron (quoting Wittgenstein), *Disarming Beauty: Essays on Faith, Truth, and Freedom* (Notre Dame, IN: University of Notre Dame Press, 2017), 128.

in Egypt. God Himself, the God of Abraham, Isaac, and Jacob, *comes down* to meet Moses. "And I have come down to deliver them out of the hand of the Egyptians, and to bring them up out of that land to a good and broad land, a land flowing with milk and honey" (Exod. 3:8).

God led the Israelites from within a column of smoke by day and by fire at night. God instructed Moses exactly how to build the tabernacle in which He would dwell: "And let them make me a sanctuary, that I may dwell in their midst" (Exod. 25:8).

God's divine plan of Revelation goes even further. The God of Abraham, Isaac, and Jacob who " 'dwells in unapproachable light' wants to communicate his own divine life to the men he feely created, in order to adopt them as his sons in his only-begotten Son (1 Tim. 6:16, cf. Eph. 1:4–5)."[114] God reveals Himself fully in His Son, who "is his Father's definitive Word."[115]

Like the Israelites in the desert, we are displaced, alienated pilgrims in search of our true home. And God, like the effusively generous King in the parable Jesus told, invites us to the wedding feast He has prepared for His son. Despite the fact that we have everything to gain and nothing to lose by attending the magnificent feast, we ignore the invitation and busy ourselves with our work or other worldly affairs—and some even "kill the messenger" (Matt. 22:1–14). Again, it is our fascination with the world that leads us astray. Just like the Israelites, we grumble and complain and wish we were back in Egypt with our flesh pots. And so, God sends His only Son to free us.

Our God delights in the beauty of this world, in His creation, in the vineyard, the fig tree, the Lebanon cedar, the olive

[114] CCC 52.
[115] CCC 24.

trees, and the mountains. He is an incarnate God, a God who became "sin who knew no sin, so that in him we might become the righteousness of God" (2 Cor. 5:21). Yet even though God is in all things sustaining them, and even though He is especially in Heaven, He also comes to dwell in us: "we will come to him and make our home with him" (John 14:23) through the Eucharist.

God is Being. He is what is most real. He gives everything its existence and purpose. Even though we are easily led astray and "far too easily pleased" by things that are less than real, when we participate in the Eucharist, we draw near to what is most real, the mystery upholding all reality. "By adhering to the Mystery in everything, man becomes free. It is there where he can find the satisfaction of his desire for totality."[116]

This is why the Eucharist is "source and summit" of our lives. It is Christ Himself, the source of all grace; it is communion with the Body of Christ—with the saints in Heaven, those suffering in Purgatory, and those of us who are pilgrims on earth. It is the same Christ who offered Himself on the Cross in expiation for our sins who is restoring our relationship with the Father, now as an unbloody sacrifice. We are drawn by His own Flesh and Blood into that mystical union with God that we long for and are called to. It is the sacrament of love.

As we participate in the Eucharist, we enter more and more into the communion of persons that is God's life. After conquering sin and death—opening the gates of Heaven and freeing the captives from slavery—Christ makes us members of the household of God, adopted children of the Father, and destined

---

[116] Julian Carron, *Disarming Beauty: Essays on Faith, Truth, and Freedom* (Notre Dame, IN: University of Notre Dame Press, 2017), 127.

to be once again united with Him and to behold the glory of God in Heaven:

> So then you are no longer strangers and sojourners, but you are fellow citizens with the saints and members of the household of God, built upon the foundation of the apostles and prophets, Christ Jesus himself being the cornerstone, in whom the whole structure is joined together and grows into a holy temple in the Lord; in whom you also are built into it for a dwelling place of God in the Spirit. (Eph. 2:19-22)

Fellow citizens with the holy ones and members of the house of God! This is our city, our destination, and our tribe!

The Church is both visible and invisible: the people of God, the mystical Body of Christ, the Bride of Christ, and the Temple of the Holy Spirit. Christ is the head and bridegroom of the Church. Through the Holy Spirit and the Sacraments, especially the Eucharist, we are brought into the Body of Christ and become a true community in Christ. We are brought into unity from the unity of the Father, Son, and Holy Spirit.[117] In his book *Bread That Is Broken*, Wilfrid Stinissen, O.C.D., emphasizes this point: "It is above all in and through the Eucharist that the Church becomes herself; namely, community, an icon of the community of the Trinity."[118]

God wants to be with us, to be close to us—so close that He became one of us; as St. Athanasius famously said, "God became man so man might become God." The result of this blessed exchange is that we can become divinized, "partakers of the divine

---

[117] CCC 806-810.

[118] Wilfrid Stinissen, O.C.D., *Bread That Is Broken* (San Francisco: Ignatius Press, 2020), 78.

nature" (2 Pet. 1:4). "And we all, with unveiled face, beholding the glory of the Lord, are being changed into his likeness from one degree of glory to another" (2 Cor. 3:18). The more we grow in friendship with God and live in His presence, attentive to every movement and inspiration of His Holy Spirit, the more we receive His own Body in the Eucharist, the more we enter into that sacred space of His infinite love and peace. As Dante said, "in His will is our peace."[119] The will of God is that sure foundation, the rock on which we build our home (Matt. 7:21, 24-27). The will of God—something that can be found anywhere and everywhere we are, requiring only attentiveness to the movement of His Spirit in the present moment—is our peace. And it is both the size of a mustard seed and greater than the universe. This is the Little Way.

We reflected at length on the Israelites as they wandered through the desert—with God leading them—attentively providing for their needs, and even dwelling with them, and on the fact that each of us in a way "recapitulates" the story in our own ongoing exodus toward true freedom, passing through the desert into our divine destiny.

There is a Jewish feast, a weeklong celebration called the feast of Tabernacles, or *Sukkot*. It commemorates the Israelites wandering in the desert while being upheld by God. For seven days and nights, all meals are eaten in a tent that has three sides and a ceiling made of natural materials, such as palm fronds, so they can see the night sky and be reminded of the forty years in the desert. They pray psalms of praise, welcome family members and guests, and celebrate with singing and dancing in the evenings.

What a beautiful way to rejoice in God's many gifts, His mercy and His love—sharing meals with family, friends, and neighbors, praising God and celebrating with an abundance of joy. And

---

[119] *Paradiso* 3.85.

ultimately, this is truly how we would like to live our lives—with deep gratitude for God's abundant blessings, with a welcoming hospitality in our homes, with meals and joyful celebrations that praise God and strengthen the bonds of our love—all the while remembering that we are journeying toward our true homeland.

Wisdom of St. Thérèse

The Little Way of St. Thérèse is a way of spiritual childhood, of becoming like little children (Matt. 18:3), completely trusting in God, abandoning oneself to His providence and mercy. "Jesus has shown me the only path which leads to this divine furnace of love. It is the complete abandonment of a baby sleeping without fear in its father's arms."[120] She felt that there could not be anyone who was as little or as weak as she was, yet if there were a littler soul, God "would be pleased to grant it still greater favors, provided it abandoned itself with total confidence" to His mercy.[121]

I hope that through the words of St. Thérèse and by reflecting on her Little Way—the way of humble confidence in God, of trust and love, of simplicity and "littleness," of being poor in spirit and of complete surrender to God's will—we can make our own homes places of light and peace, love, and generosity. By letting go and freeing ourselves from the many attachments and distractions of the material world and focusing on the one, good thing, we may bring ourselves, our families, and our communities closer to God.

How beautiful our homes and, more importantly, our lives would be if we had even a small portion of the love for God that St. Thérèse had! We can ask for her intercession in making our homes and our lives filled to the brim with love, mercy, and complete trust

---

[120] *Story of a Soul*, 150.
[121] *Story of a Soul*, 187.

in God. On July 17, shortly before her death, Thérèse made the prediction: "I feel that my mission is about to begin, my mission of making others love God as I love Him, my mission of teaching my little way to souls. If God answers my requests, my heaven will be spent on earth up until the end of the world. Yes, I want to spend my heaven in doing good on earth."[122]

Tip   From the Organizer

Schedule a time each week to do a quick tidy, in order to maintain the space you worked so hard to declutter and organize.

—Jacquelyn Dupuy

---

[122] *Story of a Soul*, 241.

Cultivating Your Rose Garden

1. Do we take as a source of reflection Christ's words that we cannot serve both God and mammon? Do we sometimes try to straddle both worlds? How does this choice—for God—impact our daily lives? Do we strive to detach ourselves from material things, from creatures, and most importantly, from our own will?

2. Do we value the sacraments—especially the Eucharist? Do we strive to receive Holy Communion frequently and reverently; and when we cannot receive, do we make Spiritual Communions? When we attend Mass, do we try to remain focused and avoid distractions?

3. What are some simple ways we can try to become more trusting in God, more "childlike" in the way that Christ intended? Do we hold on to control in certain situations or aspects of our lives or struggle to place them in God's hands?

Ten Lessons from The Little Way of Living with Less

1. Foster an attitude of detachment from things: "Set your minds on things that are above, not on things that are on earth" (Col. 3:2).

2. Be humble: do I really *need* all this stuff?

3. Place your trust and complete confidence in God; don't worry about money, or possessions, or any other thing! "Look at the birds of the air.... Are you not of more value than they?" (Matt. 6:26).

4. Ask the Holy Spirit for counsel and guidance and wisdom to know what things, attitudes, or creatures you need to let go of.

5. "The only good thing is to love God with all one's heart and to stay poor in spirit."[123] Practice the evangelical counsel of poverty. Get rid of excess and give generously to those in need.

6. Keep your heart alive to love! Serve others, strengthen the bonds of love, love God with all your mind, heart, and strength.

7. Organize your home by ordering everything around the centrality of God in your life.

---

[123] *Story of a Soul*, 50.

8. Be honest and simple. Avoid extravagance and all pretense.

9. Make one room beautiful!

10. Be grateful! Thank God for every blessing and every cross. Express gratitude to your family, friends, and co-workers.

About the Author

Laraine Bennett has a master's degree in philosophy and, together with her husband, Art, has co-authored five books: *The Temperament God Gave You*, *The Temperament God Gave Your Spouse*, *The Temperament God Gave Your Kids*, *The Emotions God Gave You*, and *Tuned In: The Power of Pressing Pause and Listening*. She also wrote *A Year of Grace: 365 Reflections for Caregivers*. Laraine and Art have four adult children and eight grandchildren and live in a historical community in Arlington, Virginia.

Sophia Institute

Sophia Institute is a nonprofit institution that seeks to nurture the spiritual, moral, and cultural life of souls and to spread the gospel of Christ in conformity with the authentic teachings of the Roman Catholic Church.

Sophia Institute Press fulfills this mission by offering translations, reprints, and new publications that afford readers a rich source of the enduring wisdom of mankind.

Sophia Institute also operates the popular online resource CatholicExchange.com. *Catholic Exchange* provides world news from a Catholic perspective as well as daily devotionals and articles that will help readers to grow in holiness and live a life consistent with the teachings of the Church.

In 2013, Sophia Institute launched Sophia Institute for Teachers to renew and rebuild Catholic culture through service to Catholic education. With the goal of nurturing the spiritual, moral, and cultural life of souls, and an abiding respect for the role and work of teachers, we strive to provide materials and programs that are at once enlightening to the mind and ennobling to the heart; faithful and complete, as well as useful and practical.

Sophia Institute gratefully recognizes the Solidarity Association for preserving and encouraging the growth of our apostolate over the course of many years. Without their generous and timely support, this book would not be in your hands.

www.SophiaInstitute.com
www.CatholicExchange.com
www.SophiaInstituteforTeachers.org

Sophia Institute Press is a registered trademark of Sophia Institute.
Sophia Institute is a tax-exempt institution as defined by the
Internal Revenue Code, Section 501(c)(3). Tax ID 22-2548708.